# The Wealth Creator

## Let's Talk Strategy

Published by Antonio M. Bravata

Printed in the United States of America

ISBN: 978-1-365-79474-2

# Disclaimer:

The information contained within this book will challenge your current belief structure. It will provide you with information you have never been told. The math and reality of the material within is real. Just remember as you read it is never too late to adjust your habits. Proceed only if you are ready to make a change.

-Antonio M Bravata

# Table of Contents

# The Wealth Creator

## Let's Talk Strategy

Presented By:

Wealth Creator Clinic, Inc

A Strategic Planning, Leadership and Business Coaching Firm.

Written By: Antonio M. Bravata CEO; Wealth Creator Clinic
Chairman/Founder; The Bravata Foundation

"Believe nothing of what you hear, and only half of what you see."

-David Copperfield

This Book is dedicated to my life's. "Walt Disney"

-It's kinda fun to do the Impossible-

-Walt Disney

# Foreword

I want to say thank you to my family and friends. Who through the good times and my darkest of days have been my back brace. Without support and motivation, I am not sure it's possible to pick yourself up off the ground when you get knocked off your feet. There are too many people to individually thank, but you know who you are.

# Tomorrow Man

Today right now, right here you are who you are (1). Tomorrow you will be who you "will" be. Each and every night, we lie down to die, and each morning we arise, reborn. Now, those who are in good spirits, with strong mental health, they look out for their Tomorrow Man. They eat right today, they drink right today, they go to sleep early today. All so that Tomorrow Man, when he awakes in his bed reborn. As Today Man, thanks Yesterday Man. He looks up fondly as a child might a good parent. He knows that someone, himself, was looking out for him. He feels cared for, and respected. Loved in words and now he has a legacy to pass on to his subsequent selves.

But those who are in a bad way, with poor mental health, they constantly leave these messes for Tomorrow Man to clean up.

They eat whatever the hell they want, drink like the night will never end, and fall asleep to forget. They don't respect Tomorrow Man, because they don't think through the fact that Tomorrow Man will be them.

So, they wake up, new Today Man, groaning at the disrespect Yesterday Man showed them. Wondering why does that guy, myself, keep punishing me? But they never learn and instead come to settle for that behavior, eventually learning to ask and expect nothing of themselves. They pass along these same habits tomorrow and tomorrow and tomorrow. And it becomes habit, psychologically genetic, like a curse.

Looking at you now, I can see exactly where you fall on this spectrum. You're constantly trying to fix today what Yesterday Man did to you. You make your bed, clean those dirty dishes from the night before, and pledge not to start drinking until six. Thinking that's the way to keep an even keel. But in reality, you're always playing catch-up.

You can't fix the mistakes of yesterday; Yesterday Man is dead. He is gone forever, and blame and atonement aren't worth a damn. What you can do is help yourself today. Eat a vegetable, read a book, cut your hair. Leave Tomorrow Man something more than a headache. Do Tomorrow Man what you would have wanted Yesterday Man to do for you.

Does that sound like a plan of action? Is this a program you think you can get with? That is strategic thinking.

Enjoy...

# Introduction

W hy money is important in the word of Dr. Drew Hennery. "Money is the means by which we may fulfill our purpose in a larger and better way. With money, we can obtain an advanced education that may aid us in the development of genius and extraordinary achievements. It gives us the leisure to devote part of our time to culture and art. Money can provide a powerful diversion for all our troubles by permitting distraction from the anxieties that assail us. With money, we can prevent ourselves from sufferings that come with poverty like cold and hunger. While sickness cannot be totally obliterated by money, it can also provide us with the satisfaction of relieving others from suffering.

To conserve wealth, we must try to get a thorough understanding of all that we may possibly do, in an honorable and legitimate way. Even to those who have inherited wealth, idleness can be a certain cause of ruin. A great fortune needs genuine labor for efficient administration. Those who leave this duty to strangers may pay a penalty for their negligence. This is why a rich man, who wants to preserve and increase his fortune, should be his own business manager. Even artists must know the price of their work. It is necessary for an artist to be a businessman, in order to have the right to be a genius. History is full of examples like this. The great Shakespeare labored as a theatre manager to obtain the necessary leisure to produce his dramatic masterpieces. Edison worked as a telegraph operator to pay the bills while he "moonlighted" as an inventor.

Everyone should, in his own way, make an effort to amass money. Some will apply money to their daily wants. Others seek to swell the fortune that they desire to leave their children. Some only desire money so they can devote it to a noble enterprise or charity. Finally, a large number see money chiefly as a means of immediate gratification. However, the main point is that no matter how much you earn, you must know how to manage your money effectively. If you cannot do so and your expenditure keeps going every month, you will not have enough to give to the causes you choose."

Thank you for reading this book. I hope it is worthwhile to you and you learn something from this. My Grandfather was a teacher, he was very big into education and after his passing, I told myself that I would carry on his role as a teacher. So that makes it my job to teach and inform you on ideas and concepts that are unfamiliar to the public. After reading this you will be able to make your own decisions in life. Like I tell everyone...it's my job to tell you what you should do, it's your job to tell me what you want to do.

Hello, allow me to introduce myself. My name is Antonio M. Bravata and over the years I have been molded by multiple people in the business world, and the education I have learned firsthand is priceless. Before we really get started and dig into the meat of things, I want to take a minute to explain how this book is laid out. We are going to cover a lot of ground here, and I want to be sure that I don't lose you along the way. I also want to make sure that it is easy for you to find the information that will be of most value to you. This book is made up of four main sections:

1. My Biography
2. Stocks and Mutual Funds
3. Investing
4. Strategic Thinking & Planning

And while each of these sections is very different, they are all extremely important as a whole. Allow me to explain, in my biography I am going to talk about who I am and how I was raised. I feel that it is impossible to fully understand what I do and how I do it if you don't know where it is that I come from. I want to share with you events that have shaped my life and molded me into who I am today. I have learned some very important lessons over the years, lessons I don't intend to forget. I want you to take the what, how, and why I do it so that you can take these ideas and make them your own. You will hear me say time and time again to not be a second-rate version of me. I want you to be a first-rate version of yourself. So, study my past and see how it has made me who I am today. Then, consider your life to find the moments that have forged you. Those are the moments that I want you to hold onto, and those are the moments you will use to drive you forward when the road gets long.

Next, I will cover investment strategies on purchasing stocks, buying companies, and investing in general. These will be the heart of why you chose to buy this book. My goal as always is to not only give you the information that will help you set sail, but it will lead to the final part of the book, and show you the "How-To" when it comes to implementing your plans. You are in control of your own future, and what you do with it is entirely up to you. So, be accountable to yourself, work smart and Carpe Diem.

*"It requires a great deal of boldness and a great deal of caution to make a great fortune, and when you have it, it requires ten times as much skill to keep it."*
-Ralph Waldo Emerson

# Biography

When I was twenty years old I wrote the first edition to this book. As time passes things change, and I believe it is important to update concepts and ideas as the decades pass. My autobiography, my story, my life as relevant to this book is laid out for you in the black and white of these pages.

Let's start with the stepping stones of my life and to do that I'm going to go back to the day I was born. As you will quickly learn, my father is one of the most important and influential figures in my life. From day one he has been my mentor and role model. I have watched him struggle, succeed and dig for every single thing he has ever had in his life. I grew up poor, grew into money and luxury, lost it all and had to rebuild. One good part about the experience for losing everything is the appreciation and the humbleness you get the second time around.

When I was little we were just scraping by. Most people tend to live paycheck to paycheck, but we couldn't even claim that much. We just lived day to day. I can remember when my dad and I would have pizza night. He always said that it was an old family recipe, although now I think maybe he learned it in his college days, which by the way would have been during this same time frame, because we are only twenty years apart. Anyways, back to the pizza recipe, a slice of bread, spread some tomato sauce, add some cheese and toast it in the oven. I mean it when I tell you we had nothing. We had lots of love and close family but financially we had nothing. My dad's father died when he was two years old leaving my grandmother to raise three infants alone, and try to put food on the table. As my dad grew up (in his twenties) he could see the life his family was facing, and he knew without a shadow of a doubt that he wanted more for us. So, he did what he had to and learned the game of money. He started his career with John Hancock. When he got the opportunity to step into a career with so much potential, he didn't bother to crawl, he just took off sprinting. When I turned eleven years old he finally got married.

Now, my dad was forced to work even harder, with a wife and a new baby on the way, again he did what he had to do and was promoted to management level. While most kids my age were watching TV, I was watching my dad. In a manner, you could say that I was learning by example. I watched how hard he worked, and how that led to the success he craved. These lessons really stuck with me, since I could see my father practicing what he preached to me. I grew up in the financial industry. It is the only thing I have ever wanted to do. By the time seventh grade rolled around, my dad was up for another promotion, this time it was to a different company; New York Life, and to a different city. At first, it was a change I was absolutely not on board with. I mean, what middle schooler is jumping for joy at the thought of leaving all their friends to go start a new life on the other side of the state? But really, in the end the change was a good thing.

This was the first time I was really forced to tread outside my comfort zone, and it allowed me to become a completely different person. You know what I'm talking about. When you grow up year after year, going to the same school and seeing the same people, you start to form a reputation for yourself. And be it good, bad, or ugly, that reputation will follow you throughout your years no matter what you do.

Moving to a new school on the other side of the state allowed me the chance to shed all of these preconceived notions. No longer was I trapped in the predetermined mold that I had fit into all my life, now I was able to present myself as the person that I wanted to be, and I took full advantage of this fact. By the time I reached high school my dad had been promoted to the head of the Greater Detroit offices of New York Life, and became a chairman council member; the highest honor in the company.

As he was growing in the industry, I was also facing my own challenges in high school. It was about this time that I learned a valuable lesson from my father. Allow me a few moments to explain.

First, I have to tell you about my love affair with the sport of football. I grew up playing the game, and I'm pretty sure my dad put a football in my hands the second I was born in the hospital in Grand Rapids, MI. the start of my senior year was here, and football twisted itself into one of the biggest roadblocks of my young life.

In all the years I had played football, I was always a starter. I always was a leader and major player on the team. I hate to say it, but it was just something that I took for granted, mainly because things had never been any other way. So, imagine my surprise when my senior year started and I found myself without a position to play. To say I was devastated would be an understatement. I mean this is my senior year we're talking about here! It was supposed to be the biggest and the best, and it was the season I had been looking forward to since I was just a little guy. I was crushed. And while I didn't realize it at the time, I was officially taking my first walk through the valley of despair.

Never heard of it? Well, while I realize that name might be new; if I can take a minute to explain for just a moment, then it may start to sound familiar. The valley of despair is a life cycle that everyone will face at some point or another. If you learn to accept the fact that the valley will always occur, you can learn how to avoid the cycle most people take, and avoid the deepest trenches. So, let's take a minute to talk about the valley.

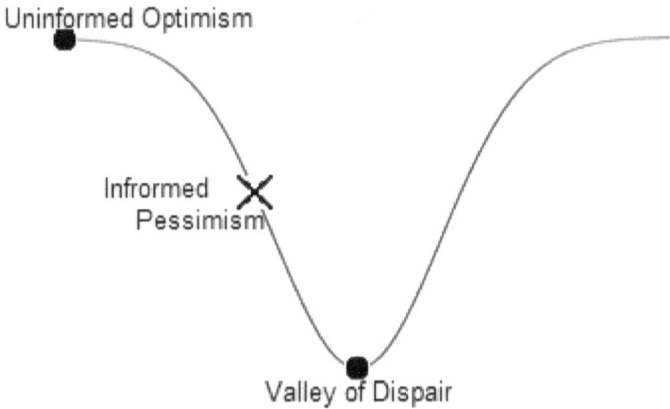

The first mark is what I call uninformed optimism. In this stage, you are ready to take on the new project or company and you are excited about the prospects. Your mind is open, your hearts engaged, and you want to tell everyone about your idea. However, it's called "uninformed" because you're so excited you forget about the road ahead. With the second step, you move into "informed pessimism."

Informed pessimism is very similar to step one, with the main difference now being, that you realize things might end up being a bit harder than you first anticipated. You are still excited about your new venture, but now the reality check says, "ok now we have to focus." the third step is the "valley of despair", and this is where things really start to get hard, because you have two choices to make (take a look at the graph below). The first choice is you say to yourself, "man, this is too hard and is getting expensive", or someone else will come to you with a new "better" idea and you quit what you're doing and repeat the process.

By the way this is the process for the majority of people. The second choice you make is to tell yourself, "I am committed to my idea and I'm not going to let anything stop Me." with this attitude you push yourself into the fourth phase, informed optimism.

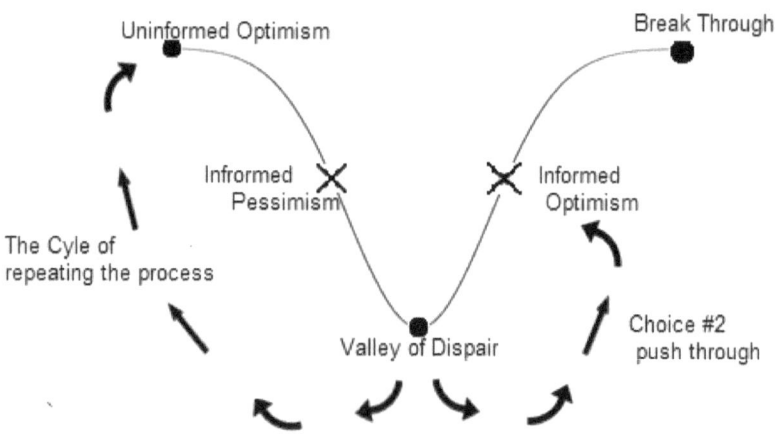

Informed optimism is where you are now alert, you know the challenges, you know the path to success and you will not let anyone take you off your path. With this route, it will lead you to the final stage, "breakthrough." When you push through to the final stage you have made your dreams a reality. Why is it so important to always push through? Simple, quitting is a habit, and once you do it the first time, it becomes that much easier to do it again...and again....and again. You get the picture.

I want you to form a different kind of habit instead. While it is never easy to find your way through the valley, it is possible. And once you do it the first time, it becomes that much easier to do it again...and again...and again. Are you starting to see the pattern?

Let's get back on track here. As I said earlier, when I found myself without a position for the start of the season, I sank quickly into the valley of despair. This was my senior year after all, and I didn't want to spend it watching quietly from the sidelines as college scouts and the crowd watched someone else play my position. So, I had a choice to make. I could give up and just sit around until it was my turn or I could make myself better. So, I pushed through and made the coaches realize they needed me in the game. By the time the second game came I was given the opportunity to start, and I wanted to seal the deal. With my opportunity, I ran a touchdown in, threw a touchdown pass, and caught a touchdown pass all in the same game. I was responsible for three touchdowns that game. That was enough to kick off my senior year.

To some people football is just a game that's played in the fall. It brightens up the sky on Friday nights, and ties up the TV over the weekend, but to me it's much more than that. It may be a game, but it is one that has taught me many lessons that I still carry with me to this day. For example, it taught me about the pain of loss. My senior year our football team had the most winningest season in my school's history, something out of a story book. We were winning every game and loving every minute of it. Then, during the last game of the regular season, on the fourth play of the game, I took a bad hit and ended up with a concussion...a bad one. I was out for a full hour, and still have no recollection of that night. Now, for those of you who have played, this may not seem like such a big deal, but it was epic to me. Mainly because I had never gotten hurt in all my years of playing. And the worst part was the next morning when my best friend came to visit me, and told me we lost.

The rest of the playoffs were like a rollercoaster. I was in and out of the valley so many times I lost count! It started when I played the next week's game against doctors' orders, and ended up with an injury that cost me a starting position. I shared time that week, and worked myself back to a starting position for the following week's game. That next week in school I tried to get out of gym class. We had a sub and our teacher was gone, but he made me participate in class. So, I tried to take it easy but as fate would have it, snap! There goes my ankle. I was on crutches for four days, and unable to practice that week.

Once again, my position was in danger so what did this mean? It meant I had to sit on the sidelines and watch my teammates play in one of the most important games of my school's history, because no other team had moved past this stage of the playoffs.

But, I wasn't about to let the valley win. So, I taped up my ankles so much I could hardly feel it, and it was not going to move. You see, no matter what life throws at you or how deep in the valley you are, you will find that there is always a way out if you want it bad enough.

After, we won that game we moved to the state semi-final, what a game! Triple overtime! We ended up losing and it absolutely sent me to the turf. It was one of the first times I experienced a loss like that. I did not like losing, and from that point forward I do everything I can to not experience loss again.

From that point, I went on to college at Northwood University, to study entrepreneurship. However, I did not finish college, I chose instead to start my career with New York Life, and get going in the business world. A year later, I started my own insurance company, a real estate company and a coaching clinic for business owners and sales representatives. I have been inducted into America's Premier Experts, which is the top twenty people hand chosen each year in their industry. At twenty years old, I made securian council from Minnesota Life, Million Dollar Round Table and was the top producer for my company for years. I have authored two books, not including this one you are now reading. By twenty-one years old I was inducted into the President's Circle at Central Michigan University and recognized as a select group of people in the honor roll of donors. My coaching clinic, the Wealth Creator Academy (now known as Wealth Creator Clinic) has helped many business owners in many different industries achieve greatness. Life is a constant experience of ups and downs and every time you see an opportunity you must take advantage of it immediately.

Entrepreneurs and high net worth individuals have chosen to work with me because of my vision for the future and my creative ideas for success. What this means to you is that I will help you step away from the institutional imperative and create a better future for yourself, while also helping bridge your opportunities into reality. The real benefit is the confidence, certainty and peace of mind in knowing you are building the life you always dreamed possible.

*"The use of all money is all the advantage there is in having money."*
*-Benjamin Franklin*

# Belief Systems

I would like to start this book with talking about our belief systems and mindsets. Your belief systems are instilled into you from day one by your parents, families, friends, and the environments you surround yourself with. They are the rules to which you live your life, and pass on to your own children. The question is; where do we get our belief systems about money?

I would like to start by telling a story of when I was a kid. I grew up in a Catholic school and we went to church twice a week. After a while I asked my dad, "Why are we catholic?" he responded by saying, "Well were catholic because your grandmother raised me that way." It was as simple as that. I could have just as easily been Mormon, Protestant, Seventh Day Adventist, Muslim, or any of the other religious. What I have noticed is it's the same with life stance, world view, politics, philosophy, any ideology. You could have a specific belief for each of those categories. This is perfectly normal. Chances are if our parents are Catholic then, we will most likely be Catholic. It is the exception rather than the rule for someone to break away and go their own way. But while it may be an exception, it's not always a bad thing!

Now, take a moment to take stock of your beliefs. After all, a big part of this chapter is about changing the belief systems that are holding you back. And how do you change something if you don't know what it is in the first place? Back to the question, where do we get our belief systems with money? Who tells us what is a good income, job, investment, etc.?

Everyone has a financial thermostat if you will; that your mind is set on. Bill Gates, Donald Trump, Warren Buffett to name a few, have thermometers that are set firmly on "B" for billions. Those individuals don't make hundreds of thousands year in and year out they make billions. Donald Trump for example can go almost personally bankrupt, file bankruptcy TWICE on two of his businesses, and almost be in the hole owing hundreds of millions. And get it all back.... when if you take yourself and your family and friends, add up all your money and probably not have as much as him? The answer is he knows how to do it. Some people's thermometers are set on "M" for millions, some are set on "100,000." Year in and year out these people will make $100,000 per year, never make $150K or $200K, but they are set at $100K. Some people are set below $100,000, where is they just cannot make six figures. The main reason is because their mind won't allow it.

If you research lottery winners, you would find that regardless of the size of the jack pot, these individuals have lost their winnings in two to three years. Their mindsets on spending and investing won't change just because they win $100 million. They will find a way to spend it and be broke again. By looking at this situation, you can see that there truly is a difference in how individuals are able to work with money. The starting point doesn't seem to be that different. So, the question is, "what is it?" Here's the big secret. They have taken the time to learn how to change the way they view money.

It may sound simple, but believe me it is a lot harder than it sounds. The good news is you have the ability to change your mind. I'm not talking about making a change like starting a new year's diet, which you plan to cheat on in a month. I am talking about a real and lasting change that you will take with you the rest of your life. It may mean you need to change your career, or it may mean that you have to change the people you surround yourself with. Whatever it is, you have to commit to it if you want it to have an effect. This is not a hot and cold change; it is changing the very values of your life.

I mention people because more often than not, it is the people that you are closest to in life that are bringing you down. It may be your oldest friends, or even your family, and that is usually where the problem lies. Those closest to you are often the ones that are causing you the most problems, and severing those ties can be both painful and necessary.

For example, from time to time, I will see old friends. The problem is that I have made different choices than they did; therefore, we are at very different places in our lives. It seems that after being around them for even short periods of time, I become frustrated and have to make excuses to leave. Why? Because, I have different choices in my life and we now have different belief systems. The bonds we held in common in earlier years no longer apply. In short, our lives have taken different paths, and now there is nothing to talk about. Now, I find I can't deal with mindsets of certain people so I choose to disassociate with them. They are my own personal road blocks and ones that I have to avoid if I want to achieve the goals I've set in my life. For me this was easy because I knew the path that I wanted my life to take. What I mean by that is that the change was easy to make, but the consequences were a bit harder to accept. While I realized that my choices would force me to drift way from people I love, that doesn't mean I was pleased by the idea. Knowing change must happen does not mean you have to like it, I just mean you must accept it. Will it be easy? No! But it will be necessary if you really want your life to be different than it is today.

Let's look at the four different types of people financially and two types of mindsets that I have learned from Robert T Kiyosaki and Warren Buffett (2).

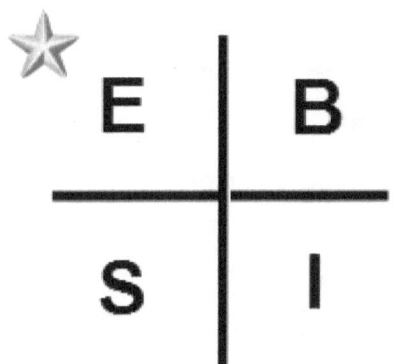

Let's start in the top left corner of the chart above labeled "E." E stands for "employee." Employees are the majority of people in the world. They give up time in exchange for security and a steady paycheck. Now, there is nothing wrong with being an employee, you can make a lot of money. However, you will never make more than the person writing your paycheck. For example, take any NFL Quarter Back. They make a lot of money however; they will never make more than their owner. And they are told when to work and how to work or they don't get paid.

Next, (in the diagram below) we move to "S." S, stands for self-employed. Most people who are employees try very hard to become self-employed. These are your doctors, lawyers, CPAs, sales agents, etc. They are no longer told when they "must" be somewhere and can set their own schedules. The other nice thing is they are the boss so they can make as much money as they want. Here is the problem with an "S." They are still employed. Yes, they are their own boss and have a company with their name on it, but if I asked you as an "S", "could you take a vacation with your family

for a few years and leave your business right now?" and the answer
will be no, this is because for a dentist to make money, he or she
needs to be in their office working on patients. Or a lawyer needs to
be in court or billing hours or there is no pay check.

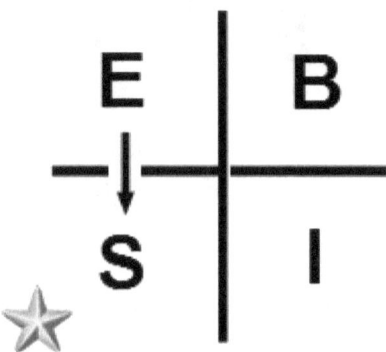

What you need to realize is that, in order for you to truly
have money, and spend time with your family or coach your kid's
games, you need to be on the right side of the line. On the right side,
if I asked a "B" and an "I" the same question as above, their answer
would be "yes!" Allow me to elaborate. Let's start with a "B".
These people are your Big Business owners. They have created a
company that generates money for them, without them being
involved. Your Donald Trumps if you will. A company that is
staffed and has a management team, and a CEO, will operate
without its founder if set up correctly. Allowing you as its owner to
take your family to Disney World and not worry if you will come
back and have money or if your company will be alive. A "B" trades
his or her safety net and security of a constant paycheck for more

risk. However, by doing so successfully, allows them all the time in the world.

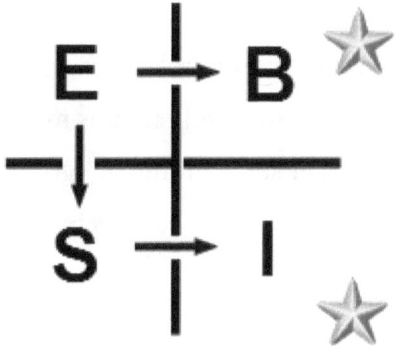

Finally, let's move on to the "I" or Investor. The investor has created a system like "B" in which their money works for itself and grows without you. Again, investors take more risk than the left side of the line, but they allow other companies who employ people on the left to use their money and make more of it. Later in the book, I will do into this case in more depth. But when I was sixteen years old, I realized how to become an "I" because my father taught me. I realized that I could go to school, play football, and have fun with my friends, while someone was going to work to pay their rent, which in turn paid for my car. A valuable lesson so early really helped mold my mind into who I am today.

(3) In closing of this chapter, I would like to talk about system 1 and system 2 thinking. It is believed that people's minds can be broken down into two modes of thought process, "quick and associative" and "slow and rule government."

System 1 is basically where you jump to an answer because it is simple and straight forward. It doesn't take much thought. For example, $1 + 1 =$?

System 2 thinking takes a little more time. It is using the reflective part of our cognition, and requires more effort to think of an answer. Remember, as I said before you have the ability to change your thinking, and you will need to in order to be good investors or big business owners.

Shane Frederick, who is the associate professor of marketing at Yale University, gathered a group of students from Harvard, Princeton, and MIT and asked these questions (4);

1. A bat and ball cost $1.10. The bat is one dollar more than the ball. How much is the ball?
2. Five machines take five minutes to make five widgets, how long would it take 100 machines to make 100 widgets?
3. In a lake, there is a patch of lily pads. Every day, the patch doubles in size. If it takes 48 days for the patch to cover the entire lake, how long will it take for the patch to cover half the lake?

I will disclose the answers in a different section of this book and go into System 1 and System 2 thinking as it relates to business. Just to help out a little, most of the Ivy League students failed to answer the questions correctly. Let's end here with a motivational type story you will see periodically throughout my book.

# The Flea

In psychology class in high school we studied fleas. A flea is quite a remarkable athlete. For its size, a flea can jump almost 5 feet in a single jump! For our experiment, we put fleas in a jar, and put a lid on the jar so they could not get out. The flea attempted many times to jump out, but every time it jumped it jumped it hit its head on the lid and was knocked down to the bottom of the jar. Now, after a while the flea gets smart, and realizes it hurts to jump so high and stopped jumping to the top.

It is here that the most amazing lesson in life is learned. You can take the top off the jar, and the flea will NEVER jump out of the jar. The flea will die of starvation and never get out. It is called "Conditioning due to Failure." You see it's not that the flea doesn't have the ability to jump out of the jar, it's that the flea no longer believes it can, therefore it won't.

Most of us are like the flea in the sense that we try to run a business or pour our hearts into taking care of our families, but something seems to always drag us down. People either give up because they have been conditioned to fail, or they learn to believe their dreams are possible and make them probable. "The opportunity for greatness will never knock on your door; it's already inside of you. You just need to let it out."-Zig Ziglar.

*"Money is the rout of all evil, and yet it is such a useful root that we cannot get on without it any more than we can without potatoes."*

*-Louisa May Alcott*

# Money in Motion

The concept of Money in Motion is not a new one, and it is one that you war probably rather familiar with already. In the section, we are going to look at how money works and how it has to keep moving if you want it to get any kind of return. Not, I am not saying that you have to constantly be moving your money, but I want you to understand how making money works on the inside. If you choose to do it yourself great! If you choose to give it to Fidelity Investments for example, my job is to show you what they do with it so you are educated. We will take this knowledge and apply it to several real-world examples in order for you to see the full reaching implications of what happens when money goes into motion. Even with something as simple as spending $50 at a gas station. You may be asking, "Why should I put my money in motion?" Well, money in motion is the one thing that creates wealth.

Let me explain how this works, even if you don't have the first investment in your portfolio. If you have a bank account then your money is already in motion. What most people don't realize is that when you make a deposit they are adding to the assets of a given bank or other financial institution. The bank then uses that money for different types of notes and loans to its members of for other types of investments.

Don't be fooled and think that your money is just sitting in a bank vault and accessible to you whenever you need it, that money is being invested, and the banks keeps the bulk of the returns and passes a small interest rate on to you for banking with them. This is how your CDs and savings accounts are able to generate interest each year. Just like any investment company, if every single investor asked to make a withdraw on their account on the same day, no bank or financial institution would be able to pay it. They would collapse.

This is why they set investment time frames of say; 1-3-5-year terms and charge a penalty if you take it out early. That money has been put in motion, and trust me when I say that bank or financial company is making plenty of money, from "borrowing" your money and keeping it moving.

While for the purposes of this book we are interested as to how this concept applies to our investments, I also want you to understand how it applies to our everyday lives as well. Our entire society is run on the principle of money in motion. Every dollar that you spend goes towards keeping our economy stable. It pays someone's salary, keeps families heat on, or feeds kids. Imagine society as a series of wheels, different sizes and spinning at different speeds, but each one connected with at least one other. All of these wheels are turning. Money is the grease that keeps things moving.

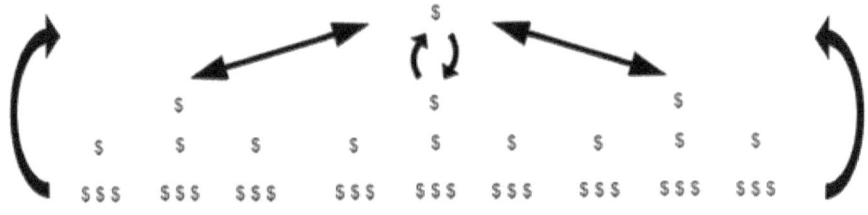

Example of Money in motion: The top dollars sign is the bank granting money to 3 people. These people buy a car, boat, and house, which spreds out to contractors, corporations, and parties. Then pay a percent back to the bank.

In the diagram above, you can see that the top dollar sign let's say is the bank who loans money to three people. Those individuals buy a car, boat, home, renovation, as the second line down (the 3 people) get the money they must now repay interest back to the bank. Meanwhile, the money they spent is being used by countless other people and companies. That is money in motion.

Eample1: for this first example let's imagine a trucking company. This is a small business, like so many in America, and let's says they employ 23 drivers. Every day before any of their drivers head off on their trek, they first stop is to a local gas station to fill up the tank. They pull out the company card and gas up the truck and then head inside for some coffee, snacks, and maybe even a magazine to flip through on a rest stop. The drivers finish up their business and head out on the road for their deliveries.

They make the journey as quickly as possible, stopping along the way for more gas, and food until they reach their destination and deliver the goods to the customers. The drivers then repeat the process as they head back home to pick up another load, and the customers pay the company for the services that they receive. While this scenario may seem simple upon first glance, when you look closer, you realize that money is moving all over the place.

First, as soon as the drivers pull into that gas station, they are sending funds off to at least half a dozen different people. They buy gas which helps the station, keep its doors open, and pay its employees. With its food purchases, it sends money to oil, and gas companies which pays their employees. That station orders more food and gas to sell which feeds the distilleries and the delivery crews. The station must also re-order magazines and drinks which helps these companies stay profitable.

Finally, think about the trucking company itself who relies on its clients to pay their invoices. If this doesn't happen then they are unable to cover their own overhead, pay their drivers, or even stay in business. And to think that all of this happens because of one small business that sends a driver in for some gas! This is what a small company can do; imagine that multiplication of every small business in America.

The same scenario is true with an individual, and investing by putting one dollar into motion it creates ripples through out our economy. Let's take a quick look at taxes for a moment. I realize no one likes to pay taxes, and please understand that I am right there with you. But let's take a look at money in motion when we do pay.

Taxes have their place in our society, and they are needed like it or not. You see, this is how the government is able to keep money in motion. They collect taxes from the population and re-disperse them across the country in various ways. Your tax dollars pay for roads, schools, hospitals, research, and parks just to name a few. They also pay for salaries, welfare for the underprivileged and emergency services.

All of these programs employ Americans, and feed families, and all require money. Think back to the Great Depression. America was in a period where the economy was so repressed that there seemed to be no end in sight. The way Roosevelt ended the Depression was to create programs that created jobs. In short, he put money into motion. The Government is not going to give up revenue. If they drop taxes in one area, they will make up the difference (and then some) in another. Therefore, if they were to drop taxes on the middle class the difference would be paid by the upper class and corporations.

Again, I realize some of you may be thinking, why is this a bad thing? I don't want to get into politics, but let's get back to money in motion. A tax break for you as an individual would probably constitute a few thousand dollars. That is extra money that you would have on hand to inject into the economy. A tax increase to your company could be in the hundreds of thousands if not millions of dollars.

This is money that they are now using to fund research, cover overhead, and pay your salary. If the taxes go up, then they will have to be paid. Belts will be tightened, and in most cases jobs will be lost. So, in a period where an economy is unstable, would you rather have a few extra thousand to put into motion, or would you choose to keep the job security and let your company keep putting money into motion.

Which do you think would have a greater effect? At this point you should understand what it means to keep money in motion. If your money is sitting then it is not growing. But that doesn't mean that I want you to just start spending! I want you to play it smart and keep your cash safe. There is a trick to this, and it is, take calculated ricks, and do your best to always protect your principal dollars. With all of the bright shiny ads that are running non-stop on TV these days, it can be tempting to jump right into a high-risk investment. After all, risk equals reward! However, you need to also look at how much you could lose, and are willing to lose.

Wealth advisors, like I used to be, are here to work with people to help find better ways to keep your money moving, and the faster the better. A little later in the book I will tell you a story of the

"Gotrock Family," which will help you learn why to avoid risk and too many advisors.

*"It isn't necessary to be rich and famous to be happy, it's only necessary to be rich."*

*-Alan Alda*

# The Macro Perspective (5)

In this chapter we are going to take a look at a wealth accumulation strategy. In short, the wealth accumulation strategy is a model that is designed to give you a visual picture of where your assets should be placed and why. You can use this model to help plan your investment portfolio and its diversification.

Step I: Vertical Diversification

If you look at the model below you will see that there are six boxes arranged in sets of two, with three rows. Each box has a letter in it, standing for "S" afe, "M" oderate, and "A" ggressive arenas. Now, the vertical arrangement of these boxes is designed to represent a game board, as to where to place your investments on the vertical diversification chart. Weather your talking to a banker, a financial planner, an insurance agent, an accountant, or a stock broker; they are all going to talk about diversification in terms of these three broad areas. And while I agree that it is a good idea to diversify in some way or another, you need to be smart about it. Thus, the point of the Wealth Accumulation Strategy.

- A = Aggressive
- M = Moderate
- S = Safe

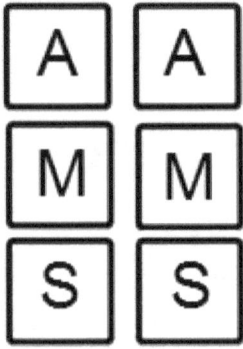

As I said above view this as your money game board. Assets you have need to be categorized in one of these main areas. Now let's move on, in the chart below I have drawn a line through our game board. Assets that are placed above the line are referred to as "paper assets." This is due to the fact that their value is not fixed. It can fluctuate constantly until the asset is actually sold. A good example of "paper assets' are your 401Ks, mutual funds, IRAs, variable annuities etc. when you look at your 401K statement your account value (which is NOT how much money you actually have, we will cover that in the next chapter) and different percentages of your portfolio that are invested into different stocks or mutual funds. What you will notice month after month is that those numbers will fluctuate depending on a number of external factors, including the market shifts. The one thing that all of these factors have in common is that they are outside of your control. Of course, we always hope that it will only go up, but the reality is that it moves in both directions.

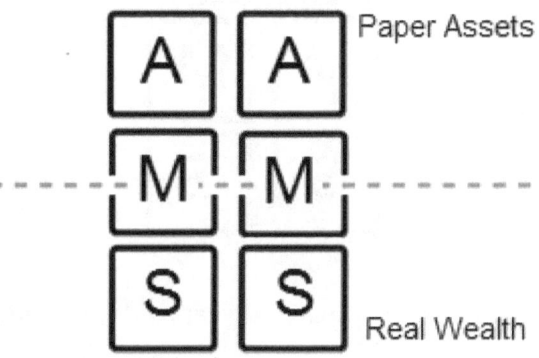

Now, I want you to look at the area below the line (see above). Assets that fall below the line are considered "Real Wealth." In other words, the values of these assets are fixed and do not fluctuate the way that assets above the line do. Examples of his would-be cash, savings accounts, and CDs. These types of fixed assets remain relatively stable and usually pay out some type of interest or dividend, but what is in the account is physical wealth, and can be cashed immediately. The decision you have to make is what percentage of your portfolio should be placed above the line, and what you want to keep below. This is called vertical diversification and the actual amounts will very base on your age, risk tolerance, and holding period. That being said, there is a direct correlation between a person's age and the percentage of their assets that fall below the line. In fact, Wall Street's rule of thumb is you would place a percentage of your assets equal to your age below the line.

This means that if you are 20 years old then you would keep 20% of your assets safe below the line and 80% above the line and more aggressive. The flip side (see above) of this strategy would be that at age 80 you would only have 20% aggressive above the line and 80% in the safe zone below the line. The reason we recommend this approach is the thought process that the younger you are, the more time you have to make up the difference, should your portfolio take a hit. The point of vertical diversification is that over time you want to slowly convert "paper assets" into "real wealth." This system works, and it is one that has been touted by experts for decades. But, there is another type of diversification to think about. This is called Horizontal Diversification; it is the diversification between tax treatments.

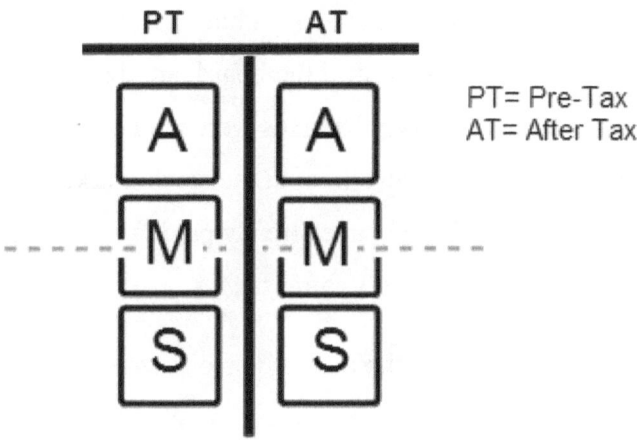

The great part about horizontal diversification is that it is fairly easy to classify your investments. This is due to the fact that there are only two types of tax treatments when it comes to savings and investments, pre-tax, and after tax. In this section, we are going to look at the difference between the two and how they relate to your portfolio. First, let's look at pre-tax investments, your 401Ks, IRAs, pension, and profit sharing plans just to name a few (see below).

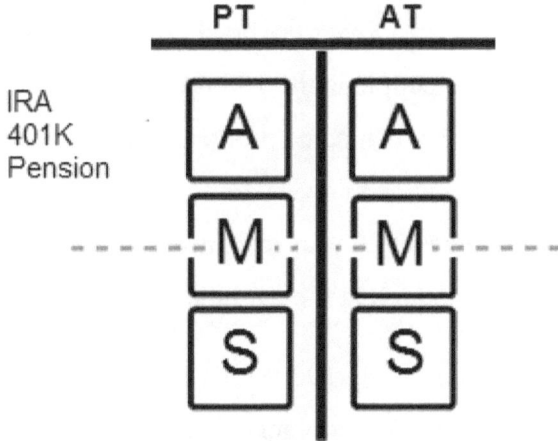

What all of these programs have in common and why they are placed in the upper left of the board, are that you have created these investments before the taxes were paid on the initial principal, and have chosen to invest them in the stock markets. Any money you invest in which you have already paid taxes on would fall on the right side of the line or AT (after tax).

For years now the mantra has been to save as much money as you possibly can in the PT category. Whether it is a 401K or an IRA, you have been told to concentrate your efforts on the pre-tax component. Advisors, companies, and even friends and family have told you to pump all the money you can into any type of pre-tax investment that you can get your hands on.

But do we know why everyone thinks that this is such a good idea? Well, if you were going all the way back to the beginning, back when these types of investments were created, you would find that people were able to defer paying taxes while in high income years, and with draw the money at retirement when they are living off less money and in a lower tax bracket. At least that was the idea. That worked for people in the 1980s retiring today in the 2009-2015. However, today that same program just will not work. The reason it is wrong today is that very few people will actually be in a lower income tax bracket 20 year from now. To understand why this is so, you first have to look at the evolution that has taken place.

Let's go back to the early 1980s for a minute. Do you have any idea what the top marginal tax bracket was back in the early 80s when these types of pre-tax plans first become popular? The top tax bracket was 70%. Not only that, but there were also 15 different tax brackets in place at the time. Back in those days if your income changed, even a little, you would move up or down a bracket or two.

At that time, people who were earning over $100,000 were in brackets over 50%. So, the mantra was that once they made it to retirement, they would live off $80,000 because, "My house is paid off, and the kids are gone, don't need $100,000 anymore." And they were right, that plan worked perfectly for the Baby Boomers retiring today. They were able to defer their taxes when they were in a 50% tax bracket and now pull it out at a 30% tax bracket. Unfortunately, today is different. Remember when I said in the 80s there were 15 different tax brackets? Well today that number has dropped to 6, the highest of which is around 35%. Also, the majority of people fall into the 15% to 25% bracket.

So, if a person, or couple, were to live off $100,000 today in 2016 and defer money, and live off $80,000 at retirement, (assuming tax brackets stay the same) how many tax brackets do they drop? I'll give you a hint; it's a big round number: zero! That's right, that $20,000 reduction in income makes absolutely no difference when it comes to the tax burden today. You would have to drop to almost 50% per year to make the old system work.

Here's the other problem with deferring money today. Are income taxes going to go up, down, or stay the same in the future? If taxes go up, you have now deferred money in a lower tax bracket to pay it out at a higher income bracket. If taxes stay the same, you lost the opportunity to invest that money today and put it in motion. With our deficits, health care issues, and all the money our country owes, my opinion is there is a no way taxes can go down, as much as I would love them to.

Have you heard anyone address this problem before? Probably not, and that's concerning as this is a very serious issue that is going to end up affecting the majority of Americans at some point in their life. So, I will ask; how can you change your actions now so to avoid this potential problem? Well, first let's go over a few different ways NOT to deal with the problem. For one thing, you don't need to go out and cancel your 401K contributions.

The pre-tax component can still be an effective and important part of your portfolio. If you can find the right balance between pre and post-tax investments you can build wealth by properly diversifying your portfolio.

Let's take a look at how this strategy can work effectively. The plan is to accumulate wealth on both sides of our game board. So, let's assume that you want to draw a retirement income from $80,000. Now this income is 100% taxable, because it stems from money you have not paid tax on. And you need to keep in mind that this money will be taxed at the current rates. Which we just discussed could be significantly higher than the rate you are paying today. But how would this situation look, if instead of drawing all

your income from the pre-tax bag, you split it up and took $40,000
from each side? (See below)

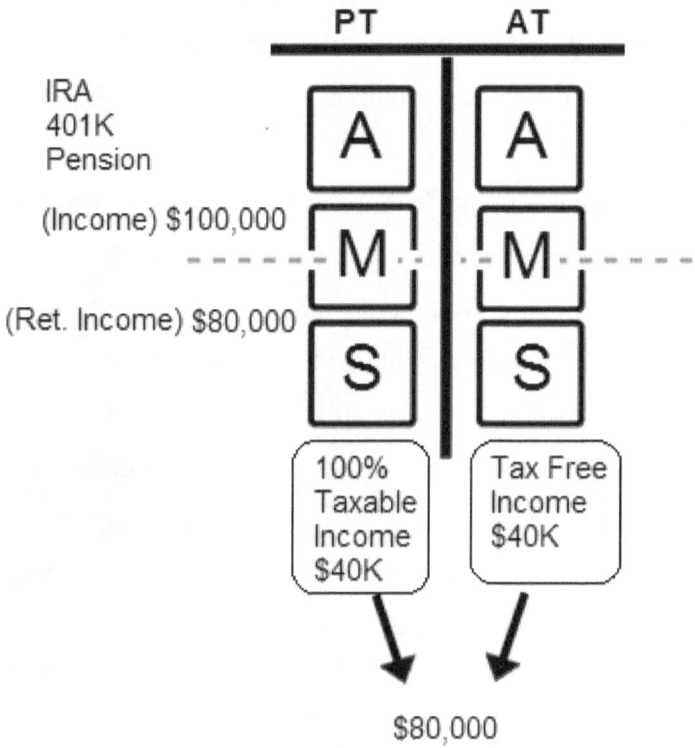

Drawing $40,000 from each side would make the amount
that you are taking from the pre-tax side of the game board
significantly smaller. Now, instead of having to pay taxes on
$80,000 annually, you only have to pay them on $40,000, while
maintaining the same $80,000 of Gross income. By using this
method now, you will drop a tax bracket, making the old way of
doing things work again. Now, let's take a look at how to set
everything up so you can accomplish this.

Let's start by placing your IRA, 401K, and Pension in the upper left box because for most people that's where it is today. But we need to work on moving it. What advantages do you know that are generally associated with below the line assets? These can include bank accounts, money market accounts, CDs, and others like this.

The main advantage is that you have liquidity. But, there are also the tax advantages. Believe it or not we do still have some pre-tax options at our disposal that hold some tax advantages. And, what these options have in common is that they all live below the line. The "Gold Standard" for this type of investment would be a tax free municipal bond. Now, what you have to think about is do you really need a tax advantage inside your PT plan? That answer would be no, because when you withdraw your income it will be taxed according to the plan, not according to the investment that you make.

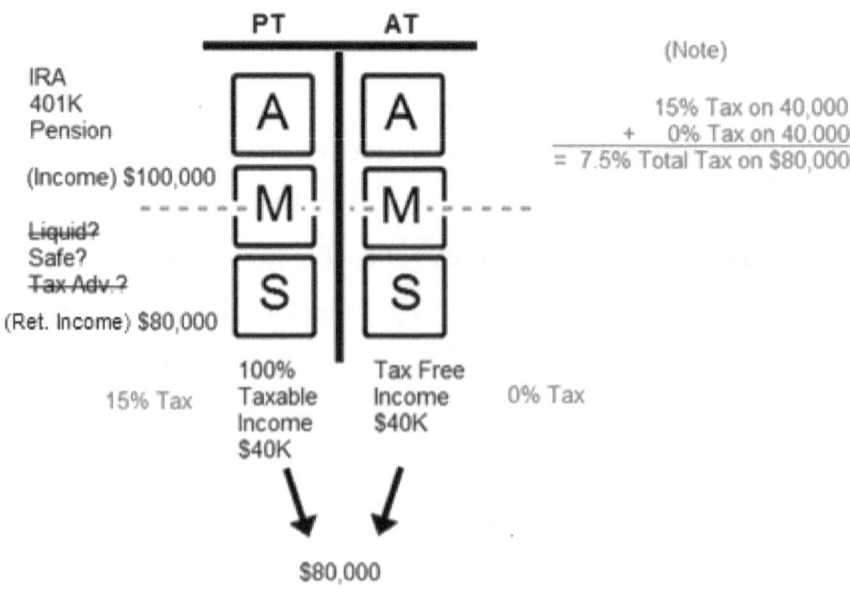

The other benefit to keeping your assets below the line was liquidity. But, do you really need liquidity inside a plan that you are not going to touch for another 20 years or so? No! Of course, you don't (see above). On to the next question, do you need safety? Well, sure you do. However, the amount of safety that you need is indirect correlation to your age. And, what kind of real "safety" do you receive when you put your money below the line? You get day to day safety, meaning that you have preservation of capital with *some* opportunity for increase. In other words, what you have in there today will be what you have tomorrow plus just a little bit more, because you can re-invest interest and dividends. But short-term safety like this is not really what you need here. Instead, let's put together a plan where you can enjoy long-term safety. The goal is for the money you are putting away today is still here 20 years from now. And if we really want to break down what it means to be "safe", then that very same money needs to have done something during that time. And that something is, it has to keep up with or exceeded the rate of inflation and technology over that time period.

Historically, the only assets that will keep pace or out preform inflation rates will be found above the line, hence the need to put your money where it can do you some good. Let's take a look at what "safety" really means above the line. If you were to chart the stock market's performance long term you would find that it has out preformed both inflation and the types of assets below the line. When we are using the pre-tax component to achieve long term objectives, we typically invest our money above the line. If you were to take a look inside your 401K plan you would find that you have several choices. These might include stocks, bonds, mutual funds, fixed interest vehicles, index funds, etc. The purpose of these funds is to help you achieve the vertical diversification that you need for your plan to be secure and profitable.

The problem with this type of diversification within a plan is that it is a micro view, looking at your PT and AT investments is at whole, is what we are after. So, the key area in our game board of the PT side is focused on the top left (see below).

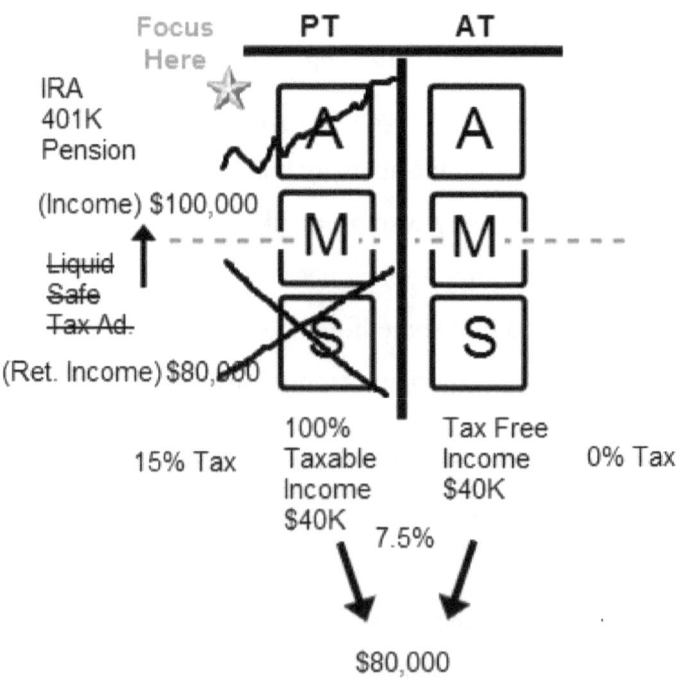

However, by focusing on the top left above the line, which leaves a problem, because now our portfolio is no longer horizontally diversified. And since achieving horizontal diversification was the very first point I made that's not good! So now let's take a moment to see how we can use the after-tax side of the game board to balance things out.

The whole point of the macro perspective and the game board is to make both sides work together in such a way as to maximize your retirement income. If your 401K represents your investment above the line, then to achieve true vertical diversification we have to take advantage of our after-tax investments by placing them below the line (see below). It turns out that all of the attributes such as safety, liquidity, and tax advantages hold a tremendous amount of value here. If you where to draw it out on our game board you would find that while PT contributions are key to the aggressive approach, AT funds are key to your "safety."

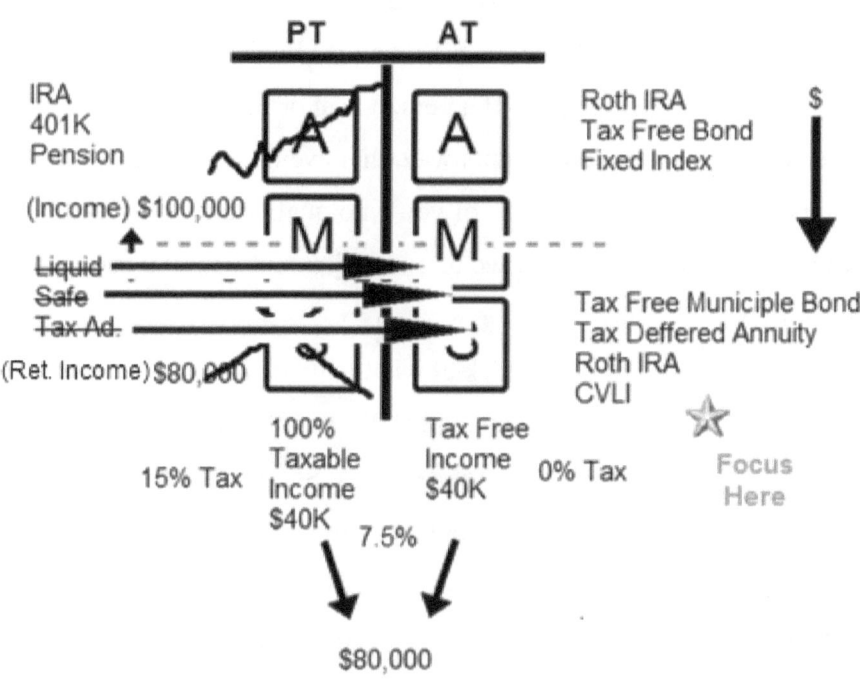

What we need to do is find a way to build a foundation below the line with tools that are capable of providing us with tax-free retirement income. Once you sift through all the garbage out there you will find just three:

1. The Roth IRA
2. Tax-Free Municipal Bonds
3. CVLI (Cash Value Life Insurance)

To be fair, there are a few other viable options that can provide income that is partially tax-free, such as a tax-deferred annuity or 529 plans. But, the real breadwinners in this category are those first three above. This is because if managed properly, they can provide future income that is completely tax free. My favorite of all investments is the CVLI or Cash Value Life Insurance. I will cover this later in another chapter. If a person is at or near retirement and wants a stream of income right away, then we might lean towards a municipal bond. But for those of you who qualify and can lock up your money until age 59 ½, we often supplement with the use of a Roth IRA.

Now we need to take a look at what realistic rates are from below the line assets. You can expect 2% to 6%, but you need to keep in mind, you don't have to pay taxes. So, it is the equivalent of 5% to 9% in the market. Even though it may seem low, remember money grows by not losing it. Of course, it won't be the 10% to 100% returns you can make going aggressive but that is not the purpose of this strategy.

Please keep in mind that many people do own AT investments that are above the line. It doesn't need to be black and white. This is just a guide to help you place your investments in a smarter manner. Remember the goal is to maximize income. One of the best after tax tools above the line would be the Roth IRA. Yes, we just saw how it can be used below the line if it needs to be, but because of its long-term nature I generally prefer to fund it with equity type investments above the line. You just need to make sure you are accumulating sufficiently in the safe area to balance the assets and permit the use of the Roth in the aggressive component.

Once we put the Roth IRA aside, when it comes to this after-tax above the line component, we aren't looking for tax free income as we were below the line. Here we are looking for sheer growth, pure and simple. Tax reduction through the use of long term capital gains is but our secondary consideration is this instance.

Now, for most people that means investing into the stock market. It might be that you choose to invest into individual stocks, common stocks, mutual funds, variable annuities, or insurance products, in the end the specific vehicle that you choose really doesn't matter. What does matter is that you obtain the "paper money" growth that you are looking for and turn it into the "real wealth" that you need for retirement. All you have to do is move the gains you receive from the aggressive side of the board to the safe side of the board. This is what I call the funnel approach. Meaning that, over time you are funneling assets down to below the line by systematic transference of assets called annual asset reallocation.

This simply means that once a year you take the time to re-balance your portfolio to get back to the ideal mix that you are striving for. Here is what that balance should look like.

You should maintain 50% of your assets above the line and 50% below the line. You may find when the year is over and your investments have moved, you are out of balance and you now have 60% above the line and 40% below. To get back in balance you would sell off 10% or take the interest or dividends and apply it below the line to reset your portfolio to 50/50.

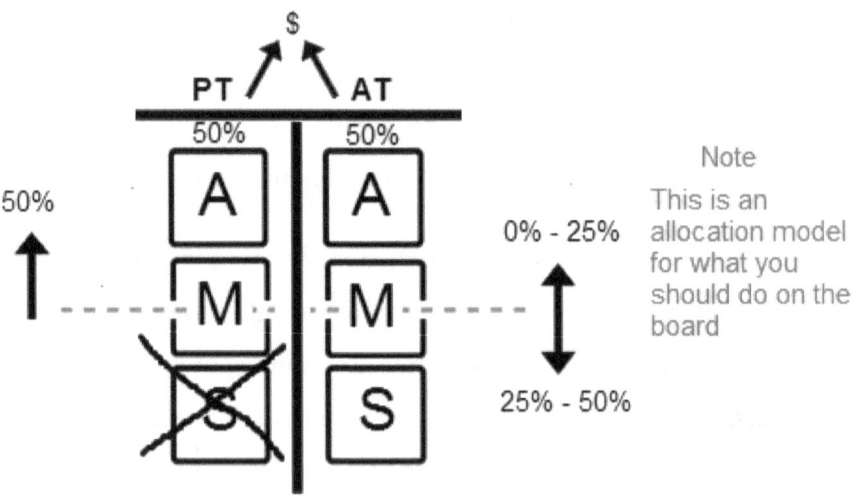

First, we need to figure out the amount of the total dollars that you have to work with. This is; we need to know all of your investable dollars. Next, divide that amount 50/50 and put half on the PT and half on the AT. And while this is a reasonable approach for many people, we have to take into account that we don't know what is going to happen to tax rates in the future.

Therefore, if we want to play it smart when we need to structure our balance in such a way that we can react to the market quickly and easily. The goal here is that you want to be able to respond to whatever the future holds quickly. Let's go into this realizing that a 50/50 split will work for most people. But real quick I want to take a few moments and explain some exceptions to the rule. If you are making $400,000 today and want to draw $300,000 per year during retirement, then you have to realize that you don't want $150,000 coming out of your PT bag. This would still keep you in a higher tax bracket, so you would want to lean more towards your AT bag for the majority of your income maybe 70/30.

The flip side to this example would be if your household income is $50,000 per year and you can live off $30,000 when you retire, if this is more your situation, the old rules still may apply to you and you could lean more off the PT bag. However, if you are the average income person then a 50/50 split is the way to go. Next, after we split 50% on the PT side and 50% on the AT side, we need to make one more split. Focusing now on the AT side (see above) you would take 50% below the line to keep an even balance. If you want to be more aggressive then you could put 0% to 25% above the line on the AT side, and keep 25% below the line. Here is an example of the allocation:

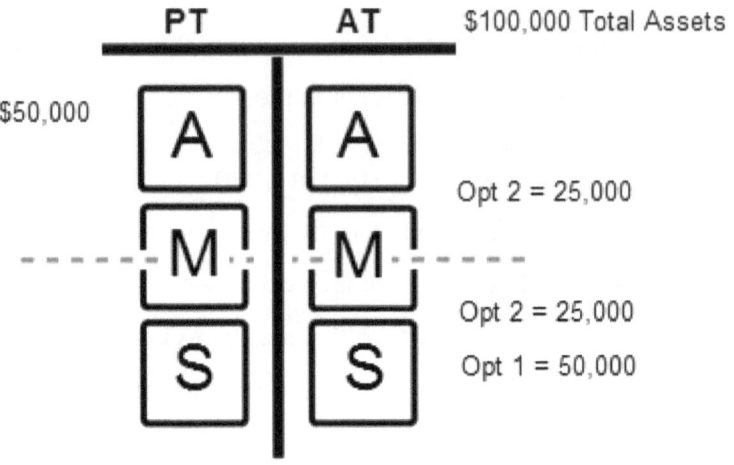

I hope this has all made sense to you and that it serves as a guide so you can use this game board strategy on your own. It will help you to be like the "Gotrock" family (I will talk about later in this book). Take the time to research your options and be the systems thinker. The first step is to get a detailed and accurate picture of all your assets, liabilities, and liquid investable income. From here put it all together on this game board and it will serve as a visual representation of your current situation you might be surprised to see how out of whack your portfolio actually is.

Finally, you will have some decisions to make. You have to decide what percentage of your investments will be put into the PT side and what percentage to add to the AT side. And don't forget to have an annual meeting with yourself to determine annual asset re-allocation. This will keep your investments in balance, as the actual value will change many times over the course of the year. Be patient with them also, trust your decisions. At the end of the day no matter how many advisors you have, you are the one in charge of your financial future. Take the time to create your strategic plan for yourself, (you will learn this later in the book) and commit yourself to it. If there were only one thing to share with you in this chapter, it would be that ANYONE with ANY income can invest. If it's even just $100, you can make magic happen. Investing, is a habit, and I realize it can be hard to start, but once you do, and you start seeing your money grow it will make you want to do more.

*"You can get anything in life you want, if you just help other people get what they want first."*

*-Zig Ziglar*

# The Story of the Volcano

I told you at random times in my book I will take a break and throw in a story. The first time I heard this one, I was listening to my dad give a presentation, and I liked it so much I had to use it. It's a fun little story that makes a perfect point when it's related to today's financial environment, which we will cover in the next chapter. So many times, we are blinded by the shiny extras, that we don't see the reality of the situation until it is too late.

Once upon a time there was a man, we'll call him Bob. And Bob had worked very hard in his life to build up his wealth so that he could have the life he always dreamed of. Well, it just so happens that Bob dreamed warm, and decided that he wanted to live out his days on an island, a very warm island.

Bob's island had everything; it had beautiful women to keep him company, warm sunshine, tall palm trees, and all the fruit and wine he could ever need. It was heaven on earth. On day, Bob's neighbor from the next island over (we'll call him Jim) stopped by for a visit. At first Bob was happy to see his friend, because even though his island was perfect he still liked someone to shoot the breeze with.

But soon, Bob realized that this was much more than a standard visit. Jim asked Bob to have a seat and then delivered some startling news. "Bob", he said, "You've got to come with me right now and leave this place forever. And you can come live with me on my island, but this place isn't safe anymore." When Bob didn't respond, Jim pressed on. "Hurry Bob, we don't have much time, we must go!" Bob was dumb struck. "Jim, why would I ever leave my island?" He asked with shock in his voice. "It's my paradise! It's the perfect place that I have dreamed of my whole life."

Calmly Jim pulled out a series of charts and documents that he had brought with him. He told Bob that here was more to this beautiful island that met the eye. You see, Bob's island was actually a volcano and it was showing strong signs that an eruption was imminent. When Bob still wasn't convinced, Jim went over every piece of paper again and again until Bob was as white as the paper. "Bob, I know this may come to a shock, but don't worry, I have room for you on my island, you will be fine," said Jim.

After a few minutes, he asked Jim to describe his island. Bob wanted to understand his choices a bit more before deciding. Jim hung his head a bit. "Bob my island doesn't look like this one. There are no beautiful girls, no swaying palm trees. I don't even have a beach. That's why I always come visit you. My island is really just a mud flat, but it will keep us safe, and you will be safe, so come with me." Jim stood and waited, Bob finally got up and the two men left eh island.

How many of us have ever lived on a volcano? A situation where on the surface everything looks good and beautiful, but in reality, it's all an illusion. Before I go into the next chapter, while we are on the topic of illusions, I want to go over some illusions in the financial industry. Everyone talks about "playing the stock market." Most of the wealthiest men in the world don't have anything to do with "playing the stock market." I mean sure, they own stock in companies in the form or common stock, but they own the companies you invest into for preferred stock, which we will cover later also. So why are you told to invest in these preferred stocks when all of the major players are investing into common stock?

Take mutual funds for example, now I am not saying they are good or bad, you have to make that decision on your own. But it is my job in this book to tell you the good and the bad so you can be well educated. Here's a big illusion on how mutual funds are allowed to advertise their rates of return and how it correlates to your actual monetary growth.

Example 1:

Fund advertises 25% average, 4-year return.

Fund + 100% - 50% + 100% - 50%

| | | |

Year 1    Year 2    Year 3    Year 4

This fund has 2 years with 100% gains = 200% and two years with -50% = -100%. However, that is still a positive 100% gain over four years which equals 25% per year. Now let's put real money into the equation.

Example 2:

Fund +    100%  -    50%   +   100%   -    50%

↓         ↓          ↓            ↓

Start                                                        Finish
Invested $50,000 + $100,000 - $50,000 + $100,000 - $50,000 = $50,000

Woah! Started with $50,000, year 1 went up 100% making my account worth $100,000, year 2 lost 50% bring me back down to $50,000; year 3 goes back up 100% equaling $100,000 and year 4 minus 50% equaling $50,000. How is it possible I started at eh same dollar amount as when I finished when I finished, when this fund is telling me I made 25% per year? See you have to be careful with averages. Technically you would have lost because of the commissions you pay for the trades too. But the point is don't be fooled by the window dressing. Be a system 2 mind and make sure you know what you're getting into.

*"There is a very easy way to return form a casino with a small fortune: go there with a large one."*

*-Jack Yelton*

# Mutual Funds & Stocks

It will soon become clear I do not like investing into mutual funds. However, that does not mean that there are not good companies out there. My job is to give you the pros and cons so you are aware to make your own decisions. I would like to start with a story from Berkshire Hathaway's 2005 annual report, right from the mouth of Warren Buffet himself. It's a simple tale really, one that seems as though it were written for children rather than seasoned investors. But while the story maybe simple, the point it makes is a bit more complex. Here is his story.

How to Minimize Investment returns (6)

It's been an easy matter for Berkshire and other owners of American equities to prosper over the years between December 31$^{st}$, 1899 and December 31$^{st}$, 1999. To give a really long-term example, the Dow rose from 66 pts to 11,497 pts (guess what annual growth rate is required to produce this result; the answer is at the end of this section).

This huge rise came about for a simple reason: over the century, American businesses did extraordinarily well and investors rode the wave of their prosperity. Businesses continue to do well. But now shareholders, though a series of self-inflicted wounds, are in a majority way cutting the returns they will realize form their investments.

The explanation of how this is happening begins with a fundamental truth; with unimportant exceptions, such as bankruptcies in which some of a company's losses are borne by creditors, the most by owners in aggregate can earn between now and judgment day is what their businesses in aggregate earn. True, by buying and selling that is clever or lucky, investor A may take more than his share of the pie at the expense of investor B. and, yes, all investors FEEL richer when stocks soar. But an owner can exit only by having someone take his place. If one investor sells high, another must buy high. For owners as a whole, there is simply no magic, no showers of money from outer space that will enable them to extract wealth form their companies beyond that created by the companies themselves. Indeed, owners must earn less than their businesses can earn because of 'fictional" costs. And that's my point: these costs are now being incurred in amounts that will cause shareholders to earn far less than they historically have.

To understand how this toll has ballooned, imagine for a moment that all American Corporations are, and always will be, owned by a single family. We'll call them the Gotrocks. After paying taxes on dividends, this family -generation after generation- becomes richer by the aggregate amount earned by its companies.

Today that amount is about 700 Billion annually. Naturally, the family spends some of those dollars. But the portions it saves steadily compounds for its benefit. In the Gotrocks household everyone grows wealthier at the same pace, and all is harmonious.

But let's now assume that a few fast-talking helpers approach the family and persuade each of the family members to try to outsmart his relatives by buying certain of their holdings and selling them certain others. The helpers –for a fee or course- obligingly agree to handle these transactions. The Gotrocks still own all of corporate America; the trades just rearranged who owns what. So, the family's annual gain in wealth diminishes, equaling the earnings of American business minus commissions paid. The more that family members trade, the smaller their share of the pie and the larger the slice received by the helpers.

This fact is not lost upon these broker-helpers: activity is their friend and in a wide variety of ways, they urge it on. After a while, most of the family members realize that they are not doing so well at this new "beat-my-brother" game. Enter another set of helpers. These newcomers explain to each member of the Gotrocks clan that by himself he'll never outsmart the rest of the family.

The suggested cure: "hire a manager- yes, us- and get the job done professionally." These manager-helpers continue to use the broker-helpers to execute trades; the manager-helpers may even increase their activity so as to permit the broker to prosper still more. Overall, a bigger slice of the pie now goes to the two classes of helpers. The family's disappointment grows. Each of its members is now employing professionals. Yet overall the group's finances have taken a turn for the worse. The solution, more help of course. It arrives in the form of financial planners and institutional consultants, who weigh in the advice the Gotrocks on selecting manager-helpers.

The befuddled family welcomes this assistance. By now its members know they can pick neither the right stocks nor the right stock pickers. Why, one might ask, should they expect success in picking the right consultant? But this question does not occur to the Gotrocks, and the consultant-helpers certainly don't suggest it to them. The Gotrocks, now supporting three classes of expensive helpers, find that their results get worse, and they sink into despair. But just is hope seems lost, a fourth group- we'll call them hyper-helpers- appear.

These friendly folks explain to the Gotrocks that their unsatisfactory results are occurring because the existing helpers-brokers, managers, consultants- are not sufficiently motivated and are simply going through motions. "What," the new helpers ask, "can you expect from such a bunch of zombies?" The new arrivals offer a breathtakingly simple solution: pay more money. Brimming with self-confidence, the hyper-helpers assert that huge contingent payments in addition to, stiff fixed fees, are what each family member must fork over in order to "really" out maneuver his relatives. The more observant members of the family see that some of the hyper-helpers are really just manager-helpers wearing new uniforms, bearing sewn-on sexy names like hedge fund or private equity.

The new helpers, however, assure the Gotrocks that this change of clothing is all important, bestowing on its wearers magical powers similar to those acquired by mild-mannered Clark Kent when he changed into Superman. Claimed by this explanation, the family decides to pay up.

And that's where we are today: a record portion of the earnings that would go in their entirety to owners- if they just all stayed in their rocking chairs- is now going to a swelling army of helpers. Particularly expensive is the recent pandemic of profit arrangements under which helpers receive large portions of the winnings when they are smart or lucky, and leave the family members with all of the losses- and large fixed fees to boot- when the helpers are dumb or unlucky. A sufficient number of arrangements like this- heads the helpers, takes much of the winnings; tails, the Gotrocks lose and pay dearly for the privilege of doing so- may make it more accurate to call the family "Hadrocks."

Today, in fact, the family's frictional costs of all sorts may well amount to 20% of American business. In other words, the burden of paying helpers may cause American equity Investors, overall, to earn 80% or so of what they would earn if they just sat and listened to no one.

Long ago, Sir Isaac Newton gave us three laws of motion, which were the work of genius. But Sir Isaac's talents didn't extend to investing: he lost a bundle in the south sea bubble, explaining later, "I can calculate the movement of the stars, but not the madness of men." If he had not been traumatized by this loss, Sir Isaac might well have gone on to discover the fourth law of motion: for investors as a whole, returns decrease as motion increases.

Don't let this confuse you with the chapter of Money in Motion, which works because YOU are putting your money in motion, NOT because you are letting helper move your money for you.

Here is the answer to the question posed at the beginning of the chapter: to get very specific, the Dow increased from 65.73 to 11,497 in the 20$^{th}$ century, and that amounts to a gain of 5.3% compounded annually (not including dividends). To achieve an equal rate of gain in the 21$^{st}$ century, the Dow will have to rise by December 31$^{st}$, 2099 to –brace yourself- precisely 2,011,011.23. But I'm willing to settle for 2,000,000; 17 years into this century, the Dow has barely gained at all. Let me ask you this, how much money can you make in a lifetime? The short answer is, never more than you can earn. At one point the Gotrocks would have made more money if they had just sat at home in their rocking chairs and done nothing. That is why this book is designed so that you can do it yourself and minimize the helpers.

So now let's talk about mutual funds, I am going to show you some illusions of some major funds and then talk to you about the pros, if you must invest in them then you should know what to look for. Mutual funds tend to be the rock stars of the financial world. They are bright, shiny, have great publicity, and everyone seems to know their names. The problem with mutual funds is that such like rock stars, once you get past the flash, there isn't much there. Let's first start by talking a detailed look at two of today's well-known funds. If you decide mutual funds are the investment choice for you, then you need to be fully aware of what you are getting into.

Let's start with talking about what a mutual fund is. The short answer is it is a type of investment pool. Investors give money to a company who pools millions of dollars together to invest it all in large numbers for large returns. Investors can take their investments out most of the time whenever they want. Some funds hold you to a 1, 3, or 5-year investment holding so they have time to create wealth. By pooling a group of people's money together it allows for major stock purchases at better discounted rates. If you took your money, say $100,000 could you go buy 20% of Coca-Cola? No, however if a fund took $100,000 from a thousand people, that would give you $100,000,000 to now invest which would allow you to purchase a major part of a company.

By doing so, individual investors can have the "safety" of investing into larger more stable companies. It can also be used for real estate, bonds, franchises, emerging markets, and pretty much anything the company wants to invest in. depending on the fund managers who are in control, as the profits come in, they can choose to re-invest the profit back into the company, re-invest into other companies, or pay the money back to the shareholders in the form of dividends. On the outside this type of investment seems to be very lucrative. That is why the cumulative value of all mutual funds worldwide is estimated at roughly $30 trillion.

When it comes to your investable dollars there are two types you will hear from brokers, qualified money and non-qualified money. Real quick, qualified money is money that you have not paid taxes on, in other words you "qualify" to pay taxes on this money when you cash it in. non-qualified money is where you have already paid taxes on it, and you do "not-qualify" to pay taxes when the money is cashed in (although there maybe capital gains tax). There are many funds out here in the public market as well as private equity. We will discuss later about what to look for when buying a business and investing. While mutual funds are popular let's go into our two funds (Fund #1) and (Fund #2), and see just how the real money grows as compared to the advertised rates they tell you. David Copperfield said it best, "believe nothing of what you hear, and only half of what you see."

Actual Fund #1

According to Morning Star, here are the advertised returns of the last years for one of the largest funds in the world. This fund advertises to the public an average rate of return of .063% annually. Which is this case would be 5.7% total over all of these year (.063% x 9 = 5.7). Let's put money into this fund and see where it goes.

Initial Investment- yr. 1          $100,000

                                 ___-11%        Investment Return yr. 1

Balance Starting yr. 2             $89,000

                                 ___-11.2%      Investment Return yr. 2

Balance Starting yr. 3             $79,032

                                 ___-22.3%      Investment Return yr. 3

Balance Starting yr. 4             $61,407

                                 ___+27.3%      Investment Return yr. 4

Balance Starting yr. 5             $78,172

                                 ___+7.8%       Investment Return yr. 5

Balance Starting yr. 6             $84,269

                                 ___+7.5%       Investment Return yr. 6

Balance Starting yr. 7             $90,589

|                          |              |                         |
| ------------------------ | ------------ | ----------------------- |
|                          | +13.7%       | Investment Return yr. 7 |
| Balance Starting yr. 8   | $102,999     |                         |
|                          | +16.8%       | Investment Return yr. 8 |
| Balance Starting yr. 9   | $120,303     |                         |
|                          | -22.9%       | Investment Return yr. 9 |
| **Final Balance**        | **$92,754.10** |                       |

When you consider, the true dollar growth of your money you will see it is different. In this case we started with $100,000 and ended with $92,754.10. We lost roughly 8% when the fund ADVERTISED positive 5.7% total return annually.

Now, I would like to use an example of a very large fund which I again will not name, just to keep a positive relationship with all firms for my private consulting. Now this fund in one year posted earnings of 52.34%! That is incredible. The next year they lost -75.43%. When these agents had you on the phone they were doing their best to keep you calm, "your invested long-term don't worry!" the third year they paid 68% gain, everyone happy now? Let's see. The fund will show a positive 44.91% over those 3 years or a 14.97% average. Let's look at the actual dollar growth.

| | | |
|---|---|---|
| Balance Starting yr. 1 | $100,000 | |
| | +52.34% | Investment Return yr. 1 |
| Balance Starting yr. 2 | $152,340 | |
| | -75.43% | Investment Return yr. 2 |
| Balance Starting yr. 3 | $38,085 | |
| | +68% | Investment Return yr. 3 |
| **Final Balance** | **$63,982** | |

We lost nearly 36%! Not a gain of 44.91%.

Now that you can calculate actual returns, check your statements (go ahead take a break).

You see the problem is that, for the losses in the bad years, it is almost impossible to catch up in the good years with mutual funds. You have to consider that the percent of returns is based on the current account value and not the original investment.

Now the question is, "how can companies advertise positive historical returns when some investors are losing money?" well for one, it is a matter of averages. They calculate their returns and divide them over a simple time line. And they are not lying, but it reflects differently to individual investors. Take this for an example; let's say company A makes 10% from January 1st until December

31$^{st}$. that company will advertise its 10% for the year. Now investor A, put money into the fund on January 1$^{st}$ and left it there the entire time. So, investor A made 10%, minus fees and commissions, so maybe 8% overall. Now investor B, invested into the fund in March and left the money there until December 31$^{st}$. Investor B, because he invests later only made 6% on his money and still had the fees and commissions for a grand total of 4% for the year. However, both investor A and B are led to believe they made 10%.

Again, don't get me wrong, these are good funds out there and some people don't know how to invest and are system 1 thinkers so they would rather leave it up to a Vanguard index fund to manage the money for them and there is nothing wrong with that. However, it is my job to help educate you, so you can create wealth, and the best way to do that is to know how to see past the glitz and glamour of advertising. Now here are three simple easy rules to remember:

1. Find a place that protects your money best in the down years.
2. Find the highest rate of return, without violating rule #1.
3. If rule #1 and #2 are good, the third is, find the company with less fees, so you don't become the "Hadrocks."

Next let's move on to stocks, because stocks are a different ball game. There are preferred stocks, common stocks, short-term investing, long term investing, and shorting stocks.

Let's start with preferred stock. This type of stock is where you get an interest rate and usually some type of dividend if the company pays it. "Preferred" means that you have more protection than that of a common stock holder. In a public company on NASDAQ you buy "preferred" stock. You have no voting rights and you are along for the ride. In a private offering your investment may look like this: you get a preferred 8% annually and share in 10% of any dividend paid, you choose a term of 1, 3, and 5 years to leave your money there. If the company is failing your preferred stock would be paid back first, before the common stock holders.

Next is common stock. This is actual ownership shares of the company. You share in voting privileges and reap all the reward when there is a reward. If a company for example has a million dollars in profits and agrees to divide 10% of the profits or $100,000 to pay to the "preferred" stockholders, then the other 90% or $90,000 is divided amongst the common stock holders at whatever percentage of the company you own.

One of the major things to understand is that, by owning common stock or preferred stock, you have to go into it as if you own the business, and not a fake piece of paper. Investing into stocks without doing your research on the companies operating functions, its services, capital needs, expenses, and future growth opportunities is a major mistake. In the book (7) Intelligent Investor, Benjamin Graham wrote, "investing is most intelligent when it is most business like." You as an investor have a choice, you can take a step back from the table, review all available information and act like a business owner, or you can play the stock market like you are going to Las Vegas. For example; you can take what you usually see as the "price/value" of your stock as it floats across the stock ticker on TV, valued by some random guy trying to make a market, as the actual value or worth of your stock. Or you can look at the company's value-sheet, income, expenses, and determine your own stocks worth.

Warren Buffet says, (8) "there is no difference in owning a company or a share of it." Finally, I will end on this: invest into companies you know and fully understand, not companies that people say are "hot" right now. If you know nothing about computers and technology don't invest into those types of companies, because how can you really know its value? Next, we have short-term investors. These are people who sit in front of their computer all day long watching the stock rise and fall, and may buy and sell multiple times throughout the day or over the course of a few months. The benefit of this is always to buy at a lower price and sell at a higher price, to avoid all downturns in the market. It may look like this:

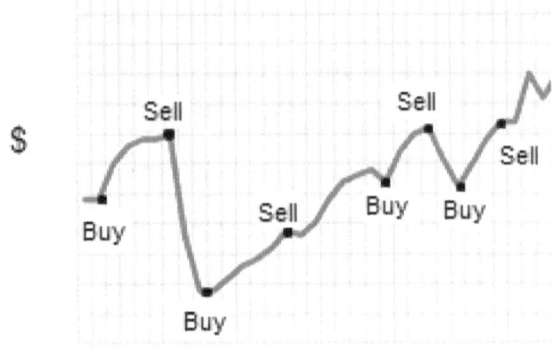

Time in the Day

The problem with this type of trading is every time you buy and sell a stock you are paying a trading fee to do so. Also, when you cash it out you will pay income tax and capital gains tax which is all deducted from your gross amount. And, most notably you lose the compounding growth rate. In essence, you have your family of "HELPERS" taking a huge piece of your pie.

The next is long term trading. These people have 10+ stocks and they will hold them for 5-10 years before selling off. These people know they won't need this money until they retire so they are willing to let it sit. They will get the compound growth of their account and only have to pay taxes once, with one trading fee and one payment to capital gains which allow you to keep a bigger piece of the pie. It may look like this:

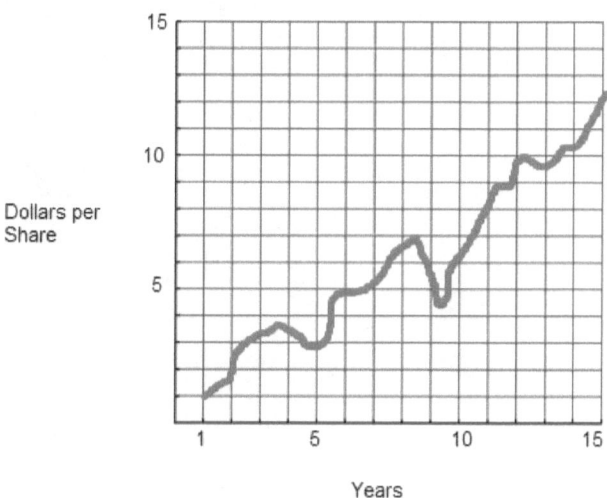

Years

This person invested at $5.00 per share and it grew to $20.00 over 10 years this would yield this person (not including dividends) 200% return but in dollars ($100,000 + 100% $5-$10 = $200,000 + 100% $10-$20 = $400,000). A $100,000 initial investment with compound growth would give you $400,000 after 10 years of which you pay one fee and taxes once.

Finally, there are many different types of strategies and ways to approach each type of stock purchase, and we will cover two main types, focus investing and shorting stocks. One thing to remember with buying stocks and going into it as you would if you were going to own the entire company, is to ask yourself; if the management is perfect for me, and the long-term growth is perfect for me, and my company is successful and would be for a while, would I sell my business today if I was asked to? Your answer should be NO! Why would you sell your company if everything is going good and the future is promising? So, then why would you sever sell a good stock? Trust your decisions and later I will show you how to put a value on a business so you know what is good and what is not.

*"Ever wonder why the IRS calls it a form 1040? Because for every $50 that you earn, you get $10 they get $40."*

*-Unknown*

# American Taxation

There is an old saying that the only two things in life that is required for you are to pay taxes and die. I always laugh at that, and just how very true it is. The reality of life in this country is that taxes are never going away. So as sad as that might make you, I can't teach you how to get out of paying your taxes. They are a necessary evil and they are here to stay weather you like it or not. However, I can teach you how to avoid unnecessary taxes.

In other words, I want you to keep as much money as you can for your family and avoid giving it away to Uncle Sam. This chapter will expose why the government allows you to invest in certain programs and how it benefits them. Before I show you an example of the taxation on your 401K and "why" the government has conditioned your mind into investing into those types of plans, we need to cover a brief history lesson.

Back when 401Ks got their start, the baby boomers where hitting the workforce. In short, a 401K is a section of the tax code that allows you to invest untaxed money and defer it to retirement years. The purpose is to put money away in your high-income years and draw the money out, to pay taxes in lower income years. It allows you to "save" taxes *this* year to effectively put more money in your pocket today. The 401K tax code was created in reaction to the decreasing number of companies that were offering pensions to their employees. Sometimes companies were purchased by investors, stripped of the pension, and then sold off, and employees would end up with nothing.

By taking part in a 401K plan it allowed the individual control of their retirement account, and no matter what happened to the company they worked for, they still got to keep their plan. The implementation of this new tax code had far reaching effects within our society, but probably the most visible effect was the boom of the stock market, due to the influx of money into the investment plans by the individual employees. On the flip side, today we are seeing the stock market's reaction to the baby boomers retiring and drawing the money form the market to live on. And there are not enough younger generation workers to add money to the market at a greater rate than is being taken out. It is this sensitivity that leads the uber-rich to shy away from preferred stock investments. They invest into and own the companies you are told to invest into, and they all own real estate.

Let's go into an example of how taxation on a 401K looks. Let's assume you are 35 years old and are going to retire at age 65. For easy math let's assume a 30% tax bracket, and you make $100,000 per year of income.

Chart

| Income | Puts 10% Away | Saves @ 30% Tax |
|--------|---------------|-----------------|
| Yr. 1 $100,000 | $10,000 | $3,000 |
| Yr. 2 $100,000 | $10,000 | $3,000 |
| | ↓ | ↓ |
| **Total added to 401K:** | **$300,000** | **$90,000** |
| | (10,000 x 30 yrs.) | (3,000 x 30 yrs.) |

Our example, he's done all the right things, he put away 10% of his income each year into his 401K. This worked out to $10,000 per year, and doing so for 30 years means he personally contributed $300,000 to his 401K plan. Because it was a 30% tax rate (we will assume rates never change) that means he "saved" $3,000 per year of taxes because he chose to put his $10,000 in a qualified plan. So, by "saving" $3,000 per year for 30 years, our example saved $90,000 over his life time in paying taxes to Uncle Sam while he was working.

Let's also assume that his 401K grew at 5.5% annually compounding for that entire 30-year span, and with company match, that his paper wealth says his 401K is worth $1,000,000. Now in retirement, our example doesn't need $100,000 per year and can live off $80,000 per year. Assuming taxes stayed the same; he will now pay $24,000 per year as he draws $80,000 of income.

## Example Chart

| Now 65 years old | Acct. Value = $1,000,000 |
|---|---|
| Income @ 8% interest | Taxes @ 30% |
| Yr.1 $80,000 | $24,000 |
| Yr.2 $80,000 | $24,000 |
| Yr.3 $80,000 | $24,000 |
| Yr.4 $80,000 | $24,000 |

**4 Year = $96,000**

Now in year 4 (use chart above) something magical happens!

It took our example 30 years of his life to put money away in the stock market, lose the ability to touch his money because it is locked in a 401K plan to save $90,000 in taxes. And in the first FOUR years, he has already paid that entire "savings" back to Uncle

Sam. But the story doesn't end there! Our example retired at age 65. Let's say he lives until age 85, so he will pay taxes of $24,000 each year for a total of 20 years. That means his overall payment to Uncle Sam is $480,000, to save $90,000 over 30 years of his working life. Again, the story doesn't end there. Our examples wife lives 7 years after her husband dies. So, she will spend the same $24,000 in taxes for 7 years, equaling another $168,000 to Uncle Sam. We are now roughly at $648,000 in taxes paid after retirement, to save $90,000! Does this sound smart to you? Well...were not done yet.

After the wife passes away that money must be passed to their children, and their kids must pay those taxes at their current tax rate. While, there are multiple transfer taxes, federal and state and you would consult an estate attorney, let's assume the kids are at the same 30% bracket. So, on 1-million-dollar estate they will pay $300,000 in taxes. That is over a million dollars paid to the government post retirement just to use a pre-tax plan and save $90,000.

The moral is that you always have to question the motives of the government or any company or any investment, to really understand why they are allowing you to invest, and what's in it for them to really make an educated decision on whether or not it's good for you. I'm not saying it's bad, I'm just saying don't go in blind. When you take the time to do the math, you will realize mutual funds and pre-tax investments are not really the best way to go in today's financial world. The unfortunate part is that many people will never realize this as they are told the opposite of what I have just showed you.

Here is another motivational story for you; this is called the Starfish. Once upon a time there was a wise man that used to go to the ocean to do his writing. He had a habit of walking on the beach before he began his work. One day he was walking along the shore, and as he looked down the beach, he saw a human figure moving like a dancer. He smiled to himself to think of someone who would dance to the day. So, he began to walk faster to catchup. As he got closer, he saw that it was a young woman and she wasn't dancing, but instead she was reaching down to the shore, picking up something and very gently throwing it into the ocean. As he got closer he called out, "Good Moring! What are you doing?" The young women paused and replied, "Throwing starfish in the ocean." "I guess I should have asked; why are you throwing starfish in the ocean?" She said, "The sun is up, and the tide is going out. If I don't throw them in they'll die." The man responded, "But Miss, don't you realize that there are miles and miles of beach, and starfish all along it? You can't possibly make a difference!"

The young women listened politely, then bent down picked another one up and threw it into the sea past the breaking waves and said, "It made a difference for that one."

My job is to coach you as an individual, or as a business owner on how to grow your business, make educated investment decisions, and structure your companies and personal lives strategically. I realize I cannot help everyone out there, but this book is designed to help the people I can. I hope after reading this book I have done my part to reach out and help throw you back into the vast ocean of business.

*"Imagination is the beginning of creation. If you imagine what you desire, you will do what you imagine and at last you create what you will."*

*-George Bernard Shaw*

# Buying a Business

In this chapter we will be going over how to buy a business and things you should look at before purchasing. We will cover how to put a value on it and calculations you will need to know when putting pen to paper. These concepts you are about to see will also help you when purchasing stock as investments.

There really is no difference in buying a company to own or in buying stock in a company. The only real difference between owing the majority of a company and owning a fraction of the company is voting privileges. When you own 51% or more of a company's stock you get to decide what happens in the company. You get to hire and decide who runs your business, determine capital allocation, and you get a better vision for the future prospects of the company.

If you own a fraction of a company's stock less than 50% your major disadvantage is you have no control, and you have less of an understanding of the company's future decisions. However, your benefits are a large quantity of companies to invest into and your ability to purchase stock at greater discounts to its intristic value. You also have the ability to get out anytime you want to. Warren Buffet says, "When investing, we view ourselves as a business analyst, not as market analysts, not as macroeconomic analysts, and not even as security analysts." (9) He chooses to use his business sense, to look at a company or stock purchase, and looks at quantitative and qualitative aspects of its management, financial positon, and its purchase price.

You should always make your investment decisions on how a company operates, and pay no mind to what market makers tell you the company is worth. Remember be a system 2 thinker and do your research. Most people believe what they hear on TV or read in the magazine written by "experts." They invest on superficial information rather than business fundamentals. In order to make it easy for you as an investor focus on businesses that you understand and are easy for you to put a value on. Second, look at its operating history and its consistency of protecting money. Remember, every company will make money in up years, which will protect your money the best in down years. Third, pay attention to the businesses future plans. Where are they going from this point today? Are they flat, have they peaked, or is there opportunity for growth?

Let's go through some principles to look at before making investment decisions in more detail (10). When it comes to asking if the business you are buying or investing into is easy for you to understand, you must know how that company actually makes its money. Don't invest into the company and not know how it generates sales. Also, what are its expenses and how does it make profit? If you don't know the details about the business, you're better off going to Las Vegas and playing black jack, you'll have better odds. If you don't fully understand it, you cannot accurately make wise decisions.

Next, if you are going to invest your family's hard-earned money into a business, you should know the companies' stocks history. Unless you are providing venture capital to a startup company, you should avoid investing into companies trying to solve difficult business problems or changing directions for the first time. If their previous plans were unsuccessful, and they are trying something new, you are investing into a maybe, and you increase your probability of a major investment error.

The problem is the media sells you on just the opposite. "A NEW CEO STEPPING IN FOR A MAJOR TURN AROUND!" "THE TECHNOLOGY GIANT STEPPING INTO THE TELEVISION INDUSTRY." These big headlines that talk about change in a good way, are really just companies that are in the midst of a corporate reorganization. People are so focused on the quick money they forget about the reality of the company's current situation. And then, we look at the long-term probability of a company's success; does your prospect have a product or service that is needed or desired? Does it have close competition? And, is it regulated? Traits like these will allow your company to create and hold its prices, without the constant fear of losing market share.

The ability to be flexible in your price point is a huge characteristic in a great business, because it creates durability and long-term probabilities that investors will be rewarded. On the flip side you have commodity type businesses. Commodity businesses have little goodwill; they sell products or services that are indistinguishable from its competitors for example, a pizza business. The only thing that can really separate one from the other is price. And as prices go down to compete, the profit margin is squeezed and hurts investors at the end. It makes investments typically low returning.

Next, let's look at the management of a company. If you are looking at company A and company B; both companies offer the same profit, some net income and literally everything is the same, how do you choose which to invest into? The answer is the management. If company A is ran by a first timer, and company B is operated by say Donald Trump, the probability of Donald Trump's business succeeding is the long-term is higher. Look at the management and see if they make rational decisions and if they make decisions that you agree with. When a mistake appears are they open and honest with you as a shareholder or do they try to hide their mistakes. The final thing to look at when it comes to management is, whether or not the management thinks for themselves or do they follow trend in the industry and mimic or copy what someone else is doing.

I was told once to be a first-rate version of myself, instead of a second-rate version of someone else. Companies often times follow trends in the industry that are doing things incorrectly, but they say to themselves, "they are doing this, so why aren't we." By doing this a company will resist change, or once a company starts making a profit and has cash, they see other companies out in the market buying others, so these "followers" will use up any available cash just to make acquisitions or start new corporate projects. One of the most detrimental things that a company will do to feel accomplished, is match salaries of another company to attract better staff or give the impression they are just as successful. Just because the CEO of company A makes a salary of $1,000,000 per year, company B feels that they must also give their CEO the same. Even though company B may not be as profitable, therefore cutting profits to shareholders.

There is an argument that a salary could be an investment into that employee, but again that is information you need to know.

It is never easy to take the road less traveled. Yet managers with strong skills should be able to persuade owners and investors to accept a short-term loss in earnings in order to help support a strategic plan that will yield superior results over time. If a manager can control their lust for activity that is unnecessary, and if they can ignore what other companies are doing and focus on their own profits. While finally being realistic about their own capabilities and keep their ego in check. The company should be "gold."

Next, let's take a look at financial principals to consider when investing in or buying a business.

First and foremost, is the focus on the return of equity and not earnings per share. Most financial analyst are trained to look at EPS (earning per share) and whether or not the EPS increased over the previous year, and did the company out preform expectations, while keeping earning high enough to be happy advertising. Warren Buffet says, "Earnings per share are a smoke screen. Most companies retain a portion of their previous years earning as a way to increase their equity base." There is nothing special about a company that increases EPS by 10%, if at the same time it is growing its earnings base by 10%. If you look at the return on equity by excluding all capital gains, losses, and any extraordinary items that may increase or decrease operating earnings, you can isolate the specific annual performance of a business. This will show you how well a company managed its returns based on the amount of capital it deployed.

By looking at a company's net income plus depreciation, depletion, and amortizations, less the amount of capital expenses and any additional work capital, you properly calculate owner earnings. Also, look for companies with high profit margins. This will tell you how well a company can control its costs, and don't overspend. As an investor or an owner this obviously just means more money in your pocket.

A quick test to calculate how well a company is doing with profit margins and creating market value is to take a company's net income, subtract all dividends paid to shareholders, and what is left is called "retained earnings." Next, add those earnings over a 10-year period. Then, determine the difference between the company's current value and its value 10 years ago. If there is an increase in the company's market value that is less than the sum of the retained earnings, the company is going backwards. However, if it has earned above average returns on retained capital, the gain in market value should exceed the sum of the companies retained earnings, which will create more than a dollar of market value for every dollar the company retained (11).

Finally, the most important question of all that you will ask when buying a business or investing in one is what is the value of the business and or the stock? There are many ways to determine a company's value. Intrinsically some are: low price to earnings ratios, low price to book values, and high dividend yields. However, the one I like was created by John Burr Williams. In his book 'The Theory of Investment Value' paraphrasing his book, he tells us that the value of a business is determined by the net cash flow expected to occur over the life of the business, discounted at an appropriate rate. Once you have the net cash flow, you can divide that by the long-term US government bond rate to give you the proper discount. Which is as close to a risk-free rate as you can get.

For example, say your net income is $100,000; next you could take it out 7-10 years putting the market value at $700,000 – $1 million and then divide the $700,000 - $1 million by the long-term percentage rate or in this case for easy math say 5%. So, your intrinsic value price would be $14,000,000. Now yes, that is a lot higher than the $700,000 - $1 million range the market says the company is worth, but remember this is how Warren Buffet determines the intrinsic value. It is a conservative way to value the future profits of a business. Let's say your $14,000,000 valuation is then divided against the total number of shares the company has. In this case, let's say 1,000,000 shares.

This means your price per share is $14.00. Your next move is to see what the market is saying the stock is worth. If for example, the market has the stock priced at $10.50 per share, which means you have the ability to purchase it at a 25% discount. To show an actual example of this in action I am going to show you a scenario form Warren Buffett in the book written by Robert Hagstrom, 'The Buffet Way' in 1973. The total market value for the Washington Post Company was $80 million. Yet Buffett claims that "most security analysis, media brokers, and media executives would have estimated WPCs intrinsic values at $400 to $500 million (12). How did Buffett arrive at that estimation? Let's walk through the numbers, using Buffett's reasoning:

| | |
|---|---:|
| WPC net income | $13,300,00 |
| Depretion & Amortization | + $3,700,000 |
| | = $17,000,000 |
| Capital Expenses | - $6,600,000 |
| 1973 Owner Earnings | = $10,400,000 |

(Next you divide these earnings by the long-term US government bond which at the time was 6.81%)

| | |
|---|---:|
| 1973 Owner Earnings | $10,400,000 |
| US Bond Rate | / 6.81% |
| | **= $152,716,593.20** |

This gives you a value of just over $150 million, almost twice the market value of the company. But well short of Buffett's $400 million to $500 million estimate. Buffett tells us that over time, the capital expenditures of the newspaper will equal depreciation and amortization charges, and therefore net income should approximate owner earnings.

Knowing this, we can simply divide net income by the risk-free rate to now reach a valuation closer to $196 million. If we stop there, the assumption is that the increase in owner earnings will equal the rise in inflation. But Buffett knew that newspapers have unusual pricing power; because most are monopolies in their community they can raise rates higher than inflation. If the WPC can raise real prices by 3% the value of the company is now closer to $350 million. He believed the manager of the WPC was determined to get the historic averages of the company back to 15% pretax margins. That would increase the total intrinsic value to $485 million. Bottom line is; there are many ways to value a company. You need to find what works best for you. However, by determining the future values you can better estimate a good price today. Once you have determined the value and correct price, the next step in buying a company or investing in a stock is to buy it at a discount to its intrinsic value.

As a rule of thumb, its best to purchase at more than 15% discount, if you are wrong on your valuation and a company's stock dips 10% you will be making a profit because of your discount to purchase price. The margin of safety also will provide you with extraordinary stock returns. If you trust your future intrinsic valuation and purchase at a 15% discount or better, the long term compounded returns will be huge.

*"Some things have to be believed to be seen"*

*-Ralph Hodgson*

# Investment Strategies

In this section I am going to cover a few investment strategies when it comes to buying common stock or preferred stock in the market. First is the "Bears" it is shorting a stock. People who love Bear markets are out there betting that a company will fail. When you are doing your valuations, and searching for a stock to buy, you may come across a company who is way overpriced. In this case, it would work the opposite of holding the stock for the long term. You will short the stock and wait for it to fail or re-correct its price to a lower price.

For example, let's say a new IPO (initial public offering) has sky-rocketed a company's stock to $1,000 per share. You know based on the math that it should be $125 a share, but because of the hype of the new offering the market is out of-whack. You can short that stock and ride it back down to $100. Putting real money into this scenario it would look like this! (See below).

| Initial Investment | Compounded Growth |
|---|---|
| $100,000 | @ $1,000 per Share |
| $200,000 | @ $500 per Share |
| $400,000 | @ $250 per Share |
| $800,000 | @ $125 per Share |

So, by investing $100,000 betting that stock would fail and re-correct to $125 per share you would have walked away with $700,000 profit due to compound growth.

The next strategy is called focus investing. Unlike most people are told, which is to "diversify" and have 20+ stocks in your portfolio it's too hard to properly manage. Focus investing means to focus on 4-5 real good stocks and deploy 80% of your portfolio to it. Once you find your 4 or 5 good companies, you hold it for the long haul. You know the old saying, "the strongest of all warriors are time and patience." – Leo Tolstoy. The majority of people frantically try to make money as quickly as possible. By doing so, they have a mistaken belief they can predict changes in the market, and while sometimes you may be right, it is just the exception as in, Las Vegas when you walk away with more than you went with, you got lucky.

Some of you may just have lost faith in long term investing due to the bear markets in 2001 and 2009. In recent years, when you encounter a strong probable opportunity you should be ready to make a large investment. In every investment, you make you should have the courage to place at minimum 10% of your net worth in it; which is also why focus investing requires only a few stocks. You should use 'Kelly optimization' to help you decide how much money to put into the investment once you determine the probability of success. Think of it like Blackjack in a casino, when the odds are strongly in your favor, you put down a bigger bet. So even though you may have 10 stocks that are good the probability of 4 of them being better means you should focus more money into those four companies.

When you choose to invest into this focus investing strategy the goal is to hold that stock for 5 – 10 years if not even for life. Think of it this way; if you are the owner of a company and you are successful today, and you have high hopes with a ton of future possibilities for growth. Would you sell your company today? Knowing in 10 years it could be worth 10 times more! Probably not.

So, when investing into a stock, go into it as if you own it. If you know the future looks better and your stock is 20% higher than when you bought into it, hold it and let the compound growth make you money. Let's talk about probabilities for a minute. Probabilities are the mathematical language for risk. What is the probability of a zebra giving birth to a dolphin? Zero, what is the probability of the sun rising tomorrow? That event, which is considered certain, is given a probability of 1. All other events that are neither completely certain nor completely impossible have a probability between 0 to 1, expressed as a fraction (11). Determining the fraction is what probability is all about. Using the Bayesian analysis (12), it allows you a way to consider a set of outcomes, by the use of information. As more information arrives you can use math to update the original probability, thus changing your decision process. Imagine this, a friend and I are playing a game and we decide to make a friendly bet. With one roll of the di, I will roll a 6.

The straight odds are 1 in 6 or 16% probability of me winning. Now, as soon as I rolled, my friend covers the results with his hand, and says, "I'll tell you it's an even number." Now that I have new information it changes the probability to 1 in 3 or 33%. He allows me to change my bet, but teases me by saying, "and it's not a 4." Now, I have a 1 in 2 or 50% probability to win. This relates to investing in that all information you can obtain about the company will help you determine the probability the company will be successful. Once, you know the probability you can implement the Kelly optimization model to help you choose how much money to invest.

However, there is one more thing about probabilities that I must mention, again coming back to a system 2 mind, you still need to take a step back from the question at hand because probabilities can be misleading at times. What I mean by this is that if you were to flip a coin 1,000 times, the outcome should be 500 heads 500 tails. Since the probability is 1 in 2 or 50%. This does not mean that it will be 50% because we all know if you flip a coin 1000 times it may be tails 800 times. So, the point is by knowing the probability, it will allow you to make better decisions, but you will should know that it is just an educated guess.

J.L Kelly a mathematician created a formula for determining optimal growth in investments, and also with gambling. Today it is called the Kelly optimization model (13). It is based on a concept that once you determine the probability of success, you bet a fraction of your bank roll that maximizes 2 times. The probability of winning (p) minus 1 equals the percentage of your total bank roll that you should bet (x) (2p-1=X). For example; if the probability of winning is 70%, you would bet 40% of your wealth or if the probability of winning is 100% you should bet 100% of your wealth. Just like any strategy there are always risks involved, and flaws with the strategy. Using the Kelly approach should help you with a long-term horizon.

The major problem you have to be careful with is, if you calculate that the probability of a stock going up, but you miscalculate that can be devastating to your portfolio. My advice would be, if you think you have a 70% chance of winning, plan on a 55% chance and be conservative, so that when you use the Kelly model, you don't over bet. Finally, to recap the 4 steps: 1. Calculate your probability, 2. Wait for the best time to buy, 3. Adjust for new information, and 4. Decide how much to invest.

*"The reality of life is your actions working their way back to you. Change your actions and you will change your reality."*

*-Antonio M. Bravata*

# Behavioral Psychology

I am not a psychologist, nor do I have a degree in a related field. However, you don't need to be a PHD to understand the emotion of winning and losing, and the emotional stress of watching something fail and having to make the choice to stop the bleeding or wait patiently for things to correct. Discomfort and emotions cause people to make rash decisions and change their normal behavior.

There are very few things in my experience that are more emotional to people than money. I have found that it is easier to talk to someone about their sex life, than their money. Especially when it's underperforming. Much of what drives people to make decisions when purchasing stocks can be explained by human behavior. And since the market is built off the collective decisions made by all stock purchasers, it would not be an exaggeration to say the market is influenced by psychological forces. When it comes to investing, people's behavior is often erratic and contradictory.

We make decisions all day long based on facts such as; we are out of milk and cereal, so we go to the store and invest in food choices for our family. We purchase homes, cars, vacations, and make decisions every minute of every day. Yet when it comes to purchasing a stock out of thousands to choose from, we panic. Most investors are unaware of their bad decisions. The study of the psychology of misjudgment is to me every bit as valuable to an investor as the analysis of a balance sheet and income statement. Benjamin Graham noted in his book 'The intelligent investor', that a person could have superior abilities in math, finance, and accounting, but if they could mot master their emotions, they would be ill suited to profit from the investment process.

Developing an investor mindset is a matter of understanding, both financially and psychologically the markets inevitable ups and downs, and to not be surprised or panic when it happens. I personally hardly ever turn on the TV and watch the stock market ticker, or the people on TV reading form a teleprompter whom are fed information. If you believe in your decisions and believe in the investment nobody should ever be able to scare you away form that decision.

However, also be aware of overconfidence. Studies have shown that errors in judgment occur because people tend to be overconfident. "This is the best company ever!" or "Man, you need to get in on this before it takes off it will be huge!" The reason for this is, because it is hard to imagine yourself as not smarter than average. Just think of a time when you have been in a room of people and you take a look around the room. You gossip with your group of friends your will and say, "man, look at all of these idiots, I bet they all think they are hot shots, only if they knew." Because in your mind you are so much better than them. Meanwhile, every other group is having the same discussion. Now don't get me wrong confidence is not a bad thing, but be careful of overconfidence. Be careful of making the big mistake of relying on information that confirms your beliefs, and disregarding information that contradicts your beliefs.

Although, I am not going to get into this, but this is most common in religion. People tend to believe information they are told that backs up their religion, but when another religion or science says something different, people tend to ignore it all.

Richard Thaler, a professor of behavioral science and economics at the University of Chicago, whose focus is questioning the rational behavior of investors. He points out several recent studies that demonstrate that people put too much emphasis on chance events. Thinking they are the exception, and they have spotted a "trend." Another mental problem investor's face is that they are more afraid of loss, than they are to welcome gains. In other words, the pain of loss is greater than the enjoyment of gain. People tend to need twice as much positive to overcome a negative. This is known as asymmetric loss aversion: the downside has greater impact than the upside. People want to be right all the time, and will hold on to a bad thing for a long to try and prove a point. And at the end of the day they lose. By not selling the losses, or admitting you were wrong, you never have to confront your failure.

(14) Consider this people in Group A were given $30 in cash and were told they had two choices: 1. pocket the money and walk away, or 2. gamble on a coin flip in which if they won they would get an extra $9. If they lost they would have $9 deducted.

Most (70%) took option 2, because they figured if they lost they would still be up $21. Those in Group B were offered a different set of choices. 1. try a gamble on a coin toss: if you win you will get $39 and if you lose you will get $21, or 2. get an even $30 with no coin toss. More than half (57%) decided to take the sure money (option 2). Both Group A & B stood the exact same chance to win the same amount of money with the exact same odds, but the situations were perceived differently.

Like I discussed in the beginning of this book, your mindset is crucial. Always take time to analyze the situation properly and try not to let emotions control you. Control your emotions. Mastering your emotions, and changing the way you think are a huge part to being a great investor and creating wealth.

*"If your ship doesn't come in, swim out to meet it".*

*-Jonathan Winters*

# Real Estate Investing

While I could write an entire book on real estate, I am only going to briefly cover some things in this chapter that will allow you some food for thought on different types of real estate projects, and some personal scenarios I have done or seen done which could help you do some things on your own. The one thing you will notice in the world of a B or an I (from the beginning of the book) is that ALL wealthy people own real estate. Why? Because like water it is the one commodity we cannot make more of. We will cover my personal experience with single family homes, discuss commercial real estate and use a scenario I have seen accomplished as well as mention a few other creative uses for properties.

First, when I was fifteen years old, I was obviously excited about getting my first car and turning 16 so I could drive on my own. So, I had approached the topic with my dad about car hunting.

After a few weeks of looking, I finally found the car I wanted. It was a black, manual transmission, Ford Mustang. Then, my dad said, "ok." Exactly the words I was ready to hear! However, those words were followed by "how are you going to pay for it?" Boom! There it was, here my dad is making a large salary at New York Life Insurance and he won't buy my car for me. So, as I was going to school, playing football and chasing girls, now I needed to find a job.

I spent weeks filling out applications, and finally got hired at the movie theater in town. After school was over I would shoot over to the theater to work until 10 PM, go home, do homework, and repeat. This lasted for three weeks, until my first paycheck. My first paycheck, after working long hours for three weeks was around $200. I remember looking at that check and feeling so mad. I almost threw the check back at my manager and said, "I think you missed a week." As soon as I got home, I told my dad, "this won't work", and then asked him to teach me how to make real money.

Over the next week or so following, he taught me real estate. I spent months looking at roughly 100 homes and found two that worked, according to a cash flow chart I had at the time. My dad explained to me, real estate investing will allow you the time you want, while someone else is paying your bills. If you find the right property and rent it at the right price.

So, after months of learning and searching, I found my first prospect single family home. That was "for sale by owner". I knocked on the door and this elderly man answered. I explained to him that I was interested in his home (I am rounding the numbers to the nearest '00 for easy math). The asking price was $110,000 and through talking to him, I found out he owed nothing on the home. The man was in his 80s and his wife had recently passed. They had lived in that home for nearly 50 years, and kept it in great shape. I then asked the man why he was selling and what he wanted to do with the money after he received it. He responded that the memories in the home were too much, and that he really didn't need all of this space just for himself. With the money he would net, he was just going to put it in a CD at a local bank and let the interest help him with his rent for his new apartment. At the time, CDs were around 5%annually.

I then quickly did the math with him and said you are asking $110,000. Let's assume after taxes you net $100,000 (giving him the benefit of the doubt) and proceed to earn 5% on that or $5,000 per year of interest. Therefore, five thousand dollars divided by twelve months is $416.66 per month. Next, I proposed my offer. I asked him if he would be willing to sell me the house, zero down on a land contract (meaning I just assume the mortgage, and make the payment to the bank, or in this scenario, the payments to him) and then I will balloon the payment in 36 months (balloon means that I must cash out the remaining purchase price at that time). I will purchase the house at the full $110,000 asking price; however, I will make payments of $600 monthly to him. Until I balloon the payments.

The benefit to him versus the outright sale is that, if he were to get all $100,000 today and earn 5% in a CD he would get $420.00 per month. In my offer, he would get $600.00 per month or $7,200 per year. That is a 2.2% increase or a total of 7.2% annual interest. Because this man was interested more in the income to help cover his new apartment rent, he accepted my offer. The next stage was to clean up the home, so that I could advertise it to a renter.

I borrowed $5,000 from my dad to fix the carpet, re-paint the home, and put an ad in the paper (which I paid back over time). After about a week, I received a phone call from a woman who was a teacher at the local college who was interested in renting the, three bedrooms, 2,000 square foot home. I gave her two options: option #1 was $1,200 monthly rent, and if there were any maintenance problems at all, she could call me, and I would be there. Options #2 was $850 per month however, she had to take care of the home and pay for any maintenance up to $10,000 in total damages (this insures the renter takes proper care of the home). The teacher chose option #2 as most people will.

At fifteen years old, I learned that a teacher (E) would go work 60 plus hours per week, to pay her rent of $850 per month to a kid. In turn, while I was out playing football, going to school, and chasing girls, she was paying my $185 per month car payment. I learned how to make my money work for me. In this scenario, she would pay me $850, I then would make a $600 payment to the man I bought the house from, and I netted $250 per month. This allowed me to pay my $185 monthly car payment and give my dad $65 per month to pay off my loan to fix up the house. The question now was; how many homes like this could I find?

This is just one example of a single-family home project that I did. There are plenty of deals like this available. It takes time and patience to find them; you will look at roughly 100 homes to find 1 that will work for you.

Next, let's move on to a commercial real estate project. The benefit of bigger projects means more money. It also can mean more headaches but that is business. Let's take a look at an outdoor strip mall. In the business, there is what's known as A-class tenants and C-class tenants. A-class tenants are your Starbucks, Dollar tree, Dick's Sports, etc. These are big business whose probability of paying the rent are very high C. C-class tenants are your mon & pop pizza shops, local clothing boutiques and local bakeries etc. These are small businesses typically a one location business that is not corporate backed. Whose ability to pay rent is based on the economy or their ability to bring people in the door.

When I am looking at buying a strip center, I am looking for those currently with A-class tenants or the locations that an A-class tenant will move to. Here is an example of a situation I have witnessed. There are multiple ways of purchasing commercial property; obviously the best way is to pay cash, however in this scenario there was a loan involved for the purchase. There was a shopping center for sale listed at $5 million. The property was half vacant with 10 units in the mall. The first thing that you need to look at is the ability to be profitable if the units were filled, by determining the rental cost per each of the 10 units based off the square footage of each. Next, you will need to see if you will be able to get those spaces leased. In this example, we were able to get A-class tenants to fill 5 of the vacant places.

The average income we can get monthly per unit in this example was $5,000 per unit. Five thousand multiplied by ten units is fifty thousand dollars monthly ($5,000 x 10 units = $50,000). However, our loan was five hundred thousand dollars per year, or forty-two thousand per month ($500,000/12 = $41,666.66). For a profit of $8,333 per month, this went to landscaping and other maintenance. Now, I know what you are thinking, by close look it appears we are not making money. In fact, we may be losing a little if we include property tax.

Also, we purchased this property at full asking price, and it looks like we are over leveraged with no equity. However, just like our focus investments, this property is not meant to be sold tomorrow, it is a long-term holding. So, let's take our income of $50,000 per month and multiply that by twelve months, and we have $600,000 ($50,000 x 12 = $600,000). Next, multiple $600,000 by 8.5 years, and you get 5.1 million ($600,000 x 8.5 = $5,100,000), so for 8.5 years I make zero dollars, but in year 9 the magic happens. My 10 tenants paid off my loan, and now I own it free and clear. My $50,000 per month is now in my pocket, and it didn't cost me a penny really to keep the property.

Again, there are many ways to structure purchases. You have cash purchases, loans from banks, investors, etc. also like our previous example; it takes time to find special deals like this. But they are out there. Notice also, there was zero profit for nearly 9 years! But that never meant there wasn't value to the purchase. Just like with your stocks, be patient and trust your long-term valuations. The final thing I would like to cover in this chapter is changing the purpose of real estate.

This can drastically change your value by really doing nothing. For example, let's say you purchase farm land for $3,000 an acre, and you buy 100 acres (3,000 x 100 = $300,000). Now that you own this property if carefully selected in the proper area, you can go to the county and change the use of the property from farming to commercial or industrial use. If you can change the zoning of the property, just out of thin air, your value has now gone up. Those 100 acres may be worth $3 million to a developer looking to build a mall, or a housing community. Think of it like this, at 100 acres, you could build 100 homes with an acre each. Let's go low and assume they only sell for $50 thousand each, that would give you $5 million (50,000 x 100 = $5,000,000). Just by being creative and having the proper zoning you can create value out of thin air. Every project will be different, and that is why real estate is fun and also why the B's and I's love real estate.

*"The problem in America isn't so much what people don't know; the problem is what people think they know that just ain't so."*

*- Will Rogers*

# CVLI

S o earlier I briefly mentioned life insurance and in my opinion life insurance is one of the best if not 'the' best investment a person can make. There is a lot of ground to cover here so I guess I will start by talking about the two basic types of life insurance.

First, term life insurance which is the most sold and advertised type of life insurance. Why do you think that is? Being a type 2 mind let's take a look at why this is. Term life gives you coverage for a very inexpensive premium for a period of time. Before eventually getting so expensive towards the end of the term that your only option is to cancel it or convert it to a whole life policy. In fact, roughly 2% of life insurance policies are actually paid out. Insurance companies get money from millions of people and then eventually later in life people forget they need it, quit paying for it, or can't afford it. It's a simple calculation which is why insurance companies "allow" you to purchase it. They know that eventually they will win. Just like a casino.

Term insurance despite the $15 a month or $15 a year payment is in reality the most expensive insurance of them all, unless you die the day you buy it. With term life there is no cash value, every dollar you add is given to the insurance company.

The next basic insurance is whole life insurance. It has many forms like 'universal' or 'variable universal' etc. But the whole life policy with a paid up additions rider is the one I want to focus on now. Whole life policies are guaranteed coverage for your life without ending on a term and if set up the way it should be, the premiums will be the same forever, with the possibilities of dividends to add to it. The real benefit however is the CVLI or cash value in the life insurance. What this means is your premiums paid into the policy are yours. You will have access to it any time throughout your life and never be penalized for taking it if you need it in the future for emergencies or whatever. Your cash value will also earn a fixed interest rate plus dividends just like any other investment. You could also set it up to mimic the markets but I would advise a fixed rate.

You see over the years insurance companies stopped promoting the actual benefits of no insurance policies and started advertising or conditioning you to use only the death benefit, which you obviously only get when you die.

What the majority of people don't realize is the true benefits for life insurance while you live. I was one of the top life insurance agents in the country working with business owners and high net worth individuals using life insurance for retirement planning, estate planning and succession planning. Now I am going to show you all the secrets one at a time so stick with me.

The purpose of this chapter is to show you the concept of the banking system, how to have your own bank so you can put money in motion for yourself.

Let's start by talking about "Human Life Value". This is a mathematical calculation so you can determine what your life is worth from a life insurance perspective. It is also a calculation we use behind the scenes to make sure we don't over insure you.

You take our age, let's say 30 years old, next take our annual income, and let's say $100,000. Average retirement as far as the calculation goes is 65 years old. So, a 30-year-old earning $100,000 will make $3.5 Million over the next 35 years. What this means is he or she should have $3.5 Million in life insurance. Why? Because, let's assume this person gets killed on their way home from work by a drunk driver. If they don't have $3.5 Million in coverage then their family gets whatever he or she does have in their investment accounts minus taxes. However, they will have financially lost the future income that they earned and would have brought into the family had they not died. So why is your life worth less if killed by a drunk driver? You should always take advantage of your life worth so your family can keep status quo, if something happens. It is a 100% probability that something will happen eventually.

Families like the Rockefellers or Kennedys or any family who generation after generation are always wealthy. They know the benefits of life insurance. If you struggle and work and live paycheck to paycheck you can leave millions of tax free money to your kids and spouse when something happens to you. You can leave a legacy and give future generations a step up in the world.

Most people think life insurance is too expensive or unnecessary but by the time I'm finished, your belief systems will hopefully have changed. Again, it's your choice, but it's my job to tell you what you should do.

One of the great benefits of life insurance is its tax free, capital gains free growth, and tax-free transfer upon ones death to their beneficiaries. It's the best "401 (k)" type option with a guaranteed finishing point, and a guarantee of principal. Where can you get that? Also, you will never have to worry about market fluctuations.

There is no such thing as having too much money. let's discuss many different options here from becoming a bank, retirement investing, protecting our company, leaving a legacy, buying your house or other type of investments from your cash value, from taking your "would be" college payments and setting up a guaranteed tax-free income in your retirement years.

Hopefully this chapter will give you a new perspective on investing and retirement in life insurance and show you how to build a cash flow system like a "B" and "I" so you can generate income without working for it.

Let's begin with the banking system. To my knowledge, created by R. Nelson Nash and his book "The Infinite Banking system", someone made the comment that if someone distributed all of the wealth in the world equally, within 10 years' time 97% of the wealth would be back under 3% of the people. Why do you think that is? I would suggest because most people don't understand banking and how interest works. Banking is probably the most important business in the world.

Without it all business would come to a standstill. Remember our money in motion talk? Whenever a transaction takes place, money flows from one party to the next. That money must come from a "reservoir" and no matter where it goes it will always end up back in the same place.

Let's take a quick example of our "401k guy" from our earlier chapter who spent his life saving $90,000 in taxes and put his money away, was penalized if he needed it, lost the opportunity to do anything with it other than pray he made money and didn't lose it. And what could have happened if he took literally the same $10,000 per year contribution and put it into his own "bank" (his whole-life insurance policy).

Our 401 (k) individual he put $10,000 away each year, or 10% of his income. Assuming he never lost money and it constantly grew at 5.5% (remember his account value at age 65 was $1,000,000). Our life insurance individual put the same $10,000 a year away. And his cash value grew just like our 401 (k) guy at 5.5% with his fixed interest and dividend payments. Aside from the cash value, he would have also had his $1,000,000 on day 1 of his plan because of the death benefit of the insurance policy.

What happens though if our 401 (k) individual dies at 40 years old, five years into his retirement plan on his way home from work, in an auto accident? Well his family would get his 401 (k) value which is around $50,000 plus whatever interest he could have made in those five years. Let's assume he did really well and he doubled his money, so he has $100,000 of value in his account. However, we now need to subtract taxes at the 30% mark so that leaves his family $70,000.

Next, the same happens to our life insurance individual. What does his family get? Well he put in the same $50,000 over those five years, and his cash value is the same $100,000 that our other person has. However, because he died, his family gets the death benefit of $1 Million dollars TAX-FREE.

They both lived the same life put the same money away collected the same interest rate over the time frame, but our life insurance person gave his family $930,000 more than our 401 (k) guy.

That doesn't seem fair, does it? That is one of the benefits to life insurance.

Now, back to life insurance as a bank, let's say you have put $100,000 away, and that's what is in your cash value. When a person buys a car, they "borrow" money from a lender and in exchange you pay an interest payment back to them for borrowing the money. So, on a $30,000 car you would make your principal plus interest payments for 36-72 months totaling maybe $45,000 with all payments combined.

The lender in essence makes $15,000 for loaning you the money. But what if you "borrowed" the $30,000 from your life insurance policy's cash value, and paid your car. Instead of just having a car paid off you paid yourself the interest payments you would be making to the lender. So, in turn you pay yourself and you will have made the $15,000 in additional payments you would have originally paid out. You can lend it to family, friends etc. and be your own bank, using your life policy.

Now, the real piece of knowledge here is that you are still earning interest on your cash value even though you borrow against it. The life insurance company loans you money against your cash value, so you're not actually using your money, which in turn allows you to still earn interest. You will be earning say 5% on your cash value and earning interest that you charge yourself or someone else to borrow from you. Putting your own money in motion to earn interest twice. Just like a bank. In case you don't know, when you lend a bank $1,000 they have $10,000 of lending power against it. That is leverage and you can do the same thing with your cash value life policy.

A beautiful way to help fund your life insurance premium so that you're not spending any more money than you currently are today is simply by funding it with your tax money. For example, let's say you make $100,000 and pay $30,000 in taxes or 30%. Every paycheck you get you would put away the 30% of that into your life policy which in turn pays for the policy. Then every year in April you would borrow back the money to pay off your taxes. The following year you repeat the process. Now, when you borrow money it creates a loan on the policy, in which you have to pay back. Remember though that the "loan" goes back to you. So technically you will always be one year behind in payments forever, unless you come up with extra money to bring it even. However, what happens if you die and you still owe yourself the $30,000? It comes off of the death benefit. So instead of getting $1 Million, your family would get $970,000.

You need to understand that you finance everything you buy in life. You either pay interest to someone else or you give up interest you could have otherwise earned. The alternate use of money must always be reckoned with; "Lost Opportunity cost". Every time you buy something or pay interest you have to calculate the lost money you could have made by not buying it. For example, instead of spending the extra $50 a month on a car because you wanted some special feature, you really lost the opportunity to invest that $50. If you would have earned ZERO interest, $50 a month for your 72-month auto loan would have been $3,600. That money at 4% interest for the 30 years you could have put it towards your retirement, which is a lot of compounded growth you lost the opportunity of earning.

So, imagine what I said earlier, by spending $9 a month on your term life policy and losing those premium payments when you could have put it to work in the whole life policy and been able to keep all of your payments. I mean $9 may not seem like much but for 30 years it adds up.

In R. Nelson Nashs book "Becoming Your Own Banker" he talks about Willie Sutton's law. It goes like this: Willie Sutton 1901-1980- was a notorious bank robber. When asked why he continues to rob banks he replied, "that's where they keep the money", so Sutton's law is formulated as; wherever wealth is accumulated, someone will try to steal it. Willie did not invent this theory; he was just a stellar practitioner.

This has been around since the beginning of time theft was the first labor saving idea. -Don't produce anything; just steal what others have produced-. Question: who is the biggest thief in the world? If you answered the internal revenue service, you would be correct. Most people feel this way but lack the understanding of why this is indeed theft. So, hers why; let's go to a shopping mall or a very public place so everyone can witness what I'm about to do. At this point I pull out a gun and place it against your head and direct you to "give me the contents of your wallet or I'll blow your brains out!" I can predict with certainty this act will be described as theft and call for punishment. But if I gather the same crowd for about an hour before you show up, and let me talk to them about how we are going to divide the contents of the wallet and give it to them, now they will call the act "democracy in action".

Frederic Bastiat 1801-1850 a French economist and statesman wrote an essay entitled "The law" in 1850:

"The law perverted! And the police powers of the state perverted along with it! The law, I say, not only turned from its proper purpose but made to follow an entirely contrary purpose! The law became the weapon of every kind of greed! Instead of checking crime the law itself, guilty of the evils it is supposed to punish! If this is true, it is a serious act, and moral duty requires me to call the attention to my fellow citizens to it."

What Bastiat saw in France in the mid-1800s and what we have today in the USA currently is "Legal Plunder". He goes on to explain "But how is this legal plunder to be identified? Quite simply: see if the law takes from some people what belongs to them, and gives it to people whom it does not belong. See if the law benefits one citizen at the expense of another by doing what the citizen himself cannot do, without committing a crime."

Willies law is active. Know today as taxes. Government is not capable of producing anything; it gets all of its sustenance from the productive element of society. It is a parasite that lives off the taxpayers.

When taxation becomes onerous to the point government sense rebellion, they resort to "exceptions of the rule." they invented qualified plans, pension plans, HR-10 plans, 401(k) plans, IRAs etc. The natural result is, the government controls everything you do, and they can and will change their minds from time to time, about every 4-8 years. They keep changing rules to give the appearance they are trying to "help" you out.

The solution would be to quit the government spending programs and get out of the lives of our citizens. But at every turn you see "financial planners" and writers that label themselves as various kinds of "financial experts" who, without exception, recommend you should participate to the fullest in your "tax-sheltered" programs. Remember our "had-rocks" these helpers came along.

In 1913 our income tax law was introduced, before our country had a surplus in the national budget and the world got along nicely. But the American people could now vote itself a benefit through its representatives in Washington and send the bill to everyone else. Such behavior leads to where we are now. "There are two methods of means and only two, whereby mans need and desires can be satisfied: 1) the production and exchange of wealth, the economic means. And 2) the uncompensated appropriation of wealth produced by others, this is the political means."-Albert J. Nock, our enemy, the state.

We all need to protect ourselves. Generation after generation keeps repeating the same old mantra, the same non-sense. Economic problems are best solved by people freely contracting with one another. Dividend paying whole life insurance has been around for 200+ years. It has stood the test of time, it is not government sponsored or backed! It is private property and protected from creditors.

If you are an individual, you can better your life. You can maximize your earnings, you can move future generations carrying your surname to the ranks of Gates, Trump, Rockefeller etc. By maximizing your Human Live Value and you can create wealth for your self today by using the same cash outlay you are today. You just need to re-direct where you want it to go.

If you own a business, here is an example of a policy I did, and how you can use it for your business. This company was valued at $50 Million and it had two partners whom owned 50% each.

What happens if one of those partners dies? Well his wife or beneficiaries would inherit his 50% share of the company. However, the problem is that person doesn't want anything to do with the business most of the time, and the partner doesn't want to work with the others beneficiary. So, what happens is they cash out the 50% equity which belongs to them. But who really loses in that case? Well one, the investors would be hurt by a 50% sell off, and two the business itself loses 50% of its value in one day. That's not good.

Especially if they have close competitors who could do a hostile takeover. So, what happens in this scenario is that I would sell both partners on the idea of purchasing a $50 Million-dollar life policy on the both of them. Now remember it won't hurt the business to pay for the policy because the 1st year cash value can be taken back and used for the business needs. Here is the big picture, partner A now dies, and the company is paid the $50 Million in life insurance tax free. $25Million or 50% of the payout belongs to partner A's family. And the additional $25 Million allows partner B to go find another partner to replace the one who died. All along the way, protecting the investors and in actuality adding to the value of the business.

It doesn't matter if your business is worth $1Million or $100 Million; you need to protect all angles. Also, if you are an elderly shareholder it creates added valuations to the business. Maybe the business alone is worth $1 Million dollars. But if the owner has made his company the beneficiary of his $1Million life policy, then anyone looking to buy the business now has added value knowing that he is going to get a guaranteed $1Million tax free bonus sometime in the near future.

Next, is an example of a university in which has a group of 4 elderly individuals who together donate $100 Million annually to the university football program. For most of you who are not familiar with large universities, it is typical that the football programs are a major part of the schools' income, which is why most money spent, is on football facilities.

So, our group of 4 alumni who have amassed a fortune over their lives are giving back. They donate $25 Million each, per year and plan on doing so for the rest of their life. So, a pitch is made to the group of people along with the university heads to set up a $25 Million policy on each of the alumni, totaling $100 Million. The purpose of doing so is that if one of these people die, the $25,000,000 is a lot of money that the school was planning on having, which now they lost. Most schools use this as a type of annuity in which they spend the money before they get it because they know it will come back to them in the next year.

But when one dies, it's a large hit, so the university pays for the policy, and again can use the cash value as needed. When one dies the $25 Million tax free money is used as a cushion so that they don't get financially hit.

In 2007, my grandfather died younger than everyone expected. For years my dad had talked to him about life insurance but he seemed to always refuse. It's hard for people to think about death, so we try to avoid it. However, the reality of death is real. When he died he left my grandmother in debt. With a very small income of her own, rental properties in disarray and for nearly 30+ years she never paid bills, or taxes, he did it all. It's a big shock.

Nothing can replace the emotional pain of death; however, the financial pain can be just as bad. For some, like my other grandmother, who never had much money because she gave and gave and gave and gave to make sure her kids and us grandkids had what we needed growing up, doesn't have much to pass on, other than memories and some personal items amassed along the journey of life. Life insurance gives people like that the ability to leave behind millions or build a church in their name, or a wing of a university with their dedication on it.

Next let's cover an investment called "viaticals", where it's basically a 3rd party owned insurance. It is an investment into someone else's life policy. As I said earlier, some who have insurance forget they need it have difficulties and can no longer afford it etc. You can find someone who is in their golden stages of life or with a medical time frame left to live or maybe they are just as healthy as can be but are in their late 70s or early 80s, but maybe they don't have much money. Let's say they have a $500,000 life policy and have a year to live. You can offer them $300,000 for example, and allow them to travel with their family and to the things in life they always wanted to do and create memories, or just maybe they want to give it to their kids or grandkids while they are alive.

They could use the money now, and maybe can't wait until later. So, you help them and in return, when the time comes you will inherit their life policy, tax free, and guaranteed. A $300,000 outlay for a $500,000 tax free return, you can't beat life insurance period. It, in my opinion, is the best investment in the world. Imagine at 20 years old, you buy a life policy on your parents, using money that you would normally have put into your 401(k) to fund it. And for your life you have peace of mind and a guaranteed retirement. Maybe when your 20, your dad is 50, so when your 65 your dad is 95 or has already gone on to a better place.

It's not something anyone wants to think of, and money isn't going to help your sadness. However, you parents, or you as a parent to your own kids, will have the confidence, certainty, and peace of mind in knowing your family is protected.

Finally, let's discuss our life insurance investments for the college aged people. Now, I am not here to bash qualified plans, mutual funds or other government sponsored plans, and I am not here to bash college. But, I want to uncover some truths and that leads me to this. Now I left college for two reasons, one, I had an opportunity to make my dreams a reality and I chose to do so. Two, the college professor I encountered in my entrepreneurship class was not who I wanted to learn from, and I feared my mindset would be changed. So, I am going to paraphrase and quote some of R. Nelson Nash's chapter in which he talks about a different look at the monetary value of a college degree. Because if I said this myself, people may just say I am bias, so I will use the words of a bestselling author.

When I was just getting established in the life insurance business we were, of course, all thoroughly indoctrinated with "needs" selling. One of those "needs" was funding for college education for the client's children. It was all assumed that the children would go to college. If there was any question as to the value on monetary terms of doing so we were taught to pint out "how much more the average college educated child would earn over a lifetime of work compared with the average child who didn't get a college degree." I forget what the figure tossed around at the time, but in recent days I was remembering the mental exercise and decided to revisit the assumption.

First of all, I have the distinct feeling that the "college degree" is extremely over-rated in its value. Witness the number of people you know who have a degree, and thus, feel they are educated but other than the degree there is very little evidence of the fact. In a recent issue of a publication at Auburn University, Dr. Herbert Rotfeld, a professor in the department of marketing and transportation had this to say:

"I entered a doctoral program because of a deep and intense curiosity, a love of learning and a pathological enjoyment of reading. Today, as an educator, I want to inspire students to learn, to teach my students so they can teach others. But since the subject of my scholarly passion is business, my students only want what they see as job certification. Many want credits but don't want to learn. Since learning requires involvement of the students who don't want to be in school. High school is something to be endured; they go to college only because a parent or school counselor told them to go. Unfortunately, as students are told to go to school, it is never emphasized that learning itself has value. Today even doctoral students go to school not to learn but to get certified, so it should not be a surprise that so many graduates at any level fail to exhibit interest or inspiration in learning. And many faculties believe that business practitioners have more credibility than anyone on campus. It is amazing how many people got into business education not because of a love of scholarship but because they were not very successful as business professionals. Now some former practitioners can be (and are) very respected scholars. Shifting from business practice to education can be a satisfying shift of career. But it is a business school, not a business. too many former business practitioners do not do any new thinking once they leave the business world, talk of training students (for the jobs they themselves once held) and demand that as business educators who 'worked' they deserve a status they never possessed in the business world. These men and women never learned to think and do not expect such strange behavior from students. It is no surprise that the graduates, like faculty, often leave with a world view as expansive as that of a pet goldfish. I await the time when business education will be a respected activity for a hard-working scholar, instead of a training ground for future anti-intellectuals and home for retired executives who came to campus so they could themselves quit thinking."

A lot of the idea that everybody needs a college education has its roots in the period just after WWII with the advent of the GI Bill. Here came the huge number of "students" to get their degrees, when the major reason for this event was the fear of government powers that "all these service men returning to civilian life are going to wreck the economy. We have to do something with them." Since that time Parkinson's Law has taken effect - a luxury once enjoyed, becomes a necessity. And so now, the cry is that "everybody 'deserves' a college education!" Please notice that the cost of doing so has risen much faster than inflation than the rest of the economy. This is always the pattern when government gets involved in anything.

So much for the major reason for looking at the value of a college degree. Now let's look at the monetary value of the college degree as compared with an alternative - teaching the child the value of learning the banking system through the use of dividend paying whole life insurance. First, I assumed that the usual cost of the college degree is $20,000 per year for four years. From what information, I can gather that seems to be the case. So, I used this same figure to put it into a high premium policy, in this case $6,500 to a base life paid up at 65 policy plus $13,500 into a paid up additions rider on an 18-year-old male. This premium total was $20,000 and was used to pay four annual premiums of $20k each. After the four years, dividends were used to pay the base premium for the duration of the policy; a classical "Premium offset".

Next, I assumed the insured retired at age 70 and surrendered dividend credits from that point on. Based on the current dividend scale of this company the cash values at age 70 were illustrated to be $2,457,303. Withdrawing dividend credits alone of $145,000 per year for retirement income that could be sustained indefinitely and tax free! And assuming the insured lived until 85 years old, means that he had withdrawn an income of $2,175,000 post retirement. If he died at that time the projected death benefit to his family is $3,279,018.

In all honesty, I don't believe that the college degree would produce comparable financial results. This scenario assumed that the insured simply let the insurance company manage the cash values throughout the entire period. By the way, if the insured was female, the above results would improve even more, in this same illustration she would have a tax-free retirement income of $150,000 per year plus a death benefit of $5,233,432 if death occurred at age 85, of course the death benefit in both cases continues to increase if death occurs later.

So, in evaluating the financial benefits of the college degree at a cost of $80,000 vs. putting the same $80,000 into a high premium whole life insurance, I don't believe the degree is as valuable. As a matter of fact, the probability of the college educated person ever learning the benefits of "banking" through the use of whole life insurance is not very good. He will be exposed to some professor teaching him that "whole life insurance is a very poor place to put money." It will take a lot of effort t to get this notion out of his head, because "unlearning" is more difficult than learning. I think that professor Rotfeld might explain it, "he has been trained instead of having learned to think". Please note that I am not against higher education. To the contrary, I believe it should be a lifelong activity. But observation leads me to conclude that we have a lot of people in America with "degrees" but not many of them are educated.

*"I never planned to fail, I just failed to plan"*

*-Unknown*

# Strategic Thinking

S trategic thinking is my coaching program that is a part of my consulting firm for business owners, and sales representatives. Over this long section, broken into subsections I am going to show you the how-to when it comes to implementation. You will leave this chapter with a new way of thinking and a model for creating your own strategic plan.

First, everything you will ever do is all about your execution. We all know people with great ideas or products. But somehow, they remain just that, ideas. Or maybe they get implemented but they never really take off and the results are not what we expected or envisioned.

Then, to our dismay, there are always those people with mediocre ideas and mediocre products that make millions. Why? Usually success comes down to two areas:

1. MARKETING

2. EXECUTION

There are many books in stores today that talk about execution; the fact is that execution is one of the key components to a successful business and strategic plan. This book is designed to help you take action, and my program has helped many individuals and organizations obtain great success. Because at the end of the day execution of the plan is what makes dreams a reality. Think of it this way, everyone in your industry is "doing" the same thing, what makes the successful ones great year in and year out is because they are "being" something else. You must find how to be you and not act like someone else.

Authentic mindsets are what attract people to you. People are so concentrated on keeping their ideas secret because they don't want other people to have them. However, what really matters is knowing you can execute the plan better. Michael Dell was asked if he was concerned that competition was duplicating his business model. He responded, "Not at all, I know I can execute it better." Even when you may have the best idea and strategy, they are worthless unless implemented correctly.

In this chapter, you will learn how to work smarter instead of working harder, believe me there is a difference. You will come to understand there is no correlation between hard work and success. I will help you raise your results by focusing on what I call "blue chip" activities and delegating "white chip" activities to someone else, by running a 13-week strategic system, you will maintain a sense of urgency to get things done on time and stay focused. If you focus your thoughts on what really drives results (blue chips), then you will become like other great individuals and great companies. They are great not because they have better products, but because they execute better than their competition.

I would like to share with you an excerpt from a fortune magazine article on "why CEOs fail; it's rarely for lack of smarts or vision. Most unsuccessful CEOs stumble because of one simple fatal shortcoming. What got Eckhard Pfeiffer fired? What fault was Bob Allen's downfall? Or Gil Amelio, Bob Stempel, John Akens, or any of the dozens of other chief executives who took public pitfalls in this unforgiving decade? Suppose what brought down all these powerful and undeniably talented executives were just one common failing? It's an intriguing question, and one of deep importance not just to CEOs and their boards, but also to investors, customers, suppliers, alliance partners, employees and many others who suffer when the top man stumbles.

The answer even matters to the country; America is the world's most competitive nation. Thanks in large part to the overall high quality of its CEOs. If people knew how to spot CEOs headed for failure, even if the company's results still looked fine, they could save themselves much pain. Trouble is; they usually look in the wrong place. Consider the Pfeiffer episode. The pundits opined, as they usually do in these cases, that the problem was with grand-scale vision and strategy.

Compaq's board removed the CEO for lack of "an internet vision"- USA Today. YEP! Agreed, the New York Times, Pfeiffer had to go because of "a strategy that appeared to pull the company in opposite directions." But was flawed strategy really Pfeiffer's sin? Not according to the man who led the coup, Compaq's chairman Benjamin Rosen said, "The change [will not be in] our fundamental strategy – we think that the strategy is sound – but in execution." Rosen said, "Our plans are to speed up decision making and make the company more efficient." You'd never guess it from reading the news or talking with your broker or studying most books, but what was true at Compaq is true at most companies where CEOs fail.

In the majority of cases (we estimate 70%) the real problem isn't the high-concept mistakes, what outside people love to talk about. It's bad execution. As simple as that: not getting things done, being indecisive, not delivering on commitments. We base our conclusions on a careful study of several dozen CEO failures we've observed over the decades, through our respective work as a consultant to major corporations and journalists covering them. The results are beyond a doubt...EXECUTION.

You see, over time things change the way business is conducted. Business models need to change with the times, yet companies don't change with it. But execution is the one component to a business model that will keep it alive. Adding a great strategic plan to the changing world around you will enhance your efforts even more. The fact remains that regardless of what industry or line of work you are in, average ideas well executed will far outweigh great ideas that are poorly implemented.

Top performers always execute better. Ever heard of the IGIG? No, because the person who created the idea failed to execute, therefore we know it today as the IPOD. Now, this is just an example but you get my point. For all of you CEOs, entrepreneurs, sales professionals, etc., in order to accomplish your goals and dreams, execution is a critical measure to your success.

The world is changing faster than ever and is moving from face to face business, to a world that competes for fast money. If you want to change with it, you must execute a new plan to perfection. Execution is simple, all it is, is following your plan into fruition.

The problem lies in completing the tasks at hand in a timely fashion. To many times we see people at year end trying to hit quotas and stressing out. So, the hard part then is finding time during your BUSY work day to accomplish what needs to get done and knowing that you are staying on track. Effective execution means that you need to be focused on taking the time to do things that will pay off at the end of the day. It means doing all you can do to rise above the day to day "white chips" and focus on a plan that will get you to your destination without taking you around the block a couple of times.

Some people think execution is easy, it just means writing down your goals and carrying them out until it's completed.

Strategic thinking is not just about completion. It is completion on time; completion and execution of strategies and tactics that focus on high payoff money making activities. It means creating visions that bring urgency to the day-to-day activities and understanding that greatness is created in this very moment, today, right now! It's about getting things done better, thinking better, dreaming better.

# -Getting Your Mind in the Right Spot-

T hinking and ideas are what drives your actions to create results; the problem is that organizations and individuals never seem to have a problem with ideas. Weather it is marketing techniques, sales ideas, cutting costs, etc., there is always more ideas than you can effectively implement. The breakdown is not in knowing but in applying.

Most people are taught to set annual goals for yourself or your company. Most people even have gone through the process where, we might examine our plan and evaluate on a quarterly basis, where we stand on our annual plan. What we have learned over the years, is that creating annual plans and goals will set ourselves up for failure, and we lengthen the gap to reach breakthrough success as individuals and as a whole. We have come to understand that annual thinking is a process that limits the performance of the entire organization. Now, I am not saying don't have annual goals.

As a matter of fact, when I get into setting a vision I will make sure that you have a three and five-year goal. However, the problem with annual planning is the mindset that is thrust upon you and your organization. It is the illusion of time, and a way to "maybe" achieve your goal, but rarely will it ever get you or your organization to break through to levels that you may or may not have ever dreamed.

When I created one of my companies, I never really dreamed up front that it would have grown to what it did. My brain did not allow the thoughts of such growth to be treated as reality. But through shifting my focus to the 13-week planning system, I was allowed to expand and move, with the events that I faced on a day to day, week to week reality. I was allowed to stretch what was impossible to make it possible. Many of you for example reading this book may wish to make $100,000 per year. Your mind may not even let you dream of making $10 million per year, or $100 million in a year, or for example spending $1 billion on a single purchase, as the CEO of Facebook did when buying Instagram in 2013.

Do you have the systems to allow you to accept the opportunities? Do you have the systems that will allow your thinking to take you to those levels?

Let's look at an example of annual thinking. At the beginning of the year you set a goal for yourself and let's assume it's a monetary goal, you want to make $100,000 this year. So, at the end of January, you see that you are a little behind your goal, but hey it's ok because it's only January. You may be a little disappointed, but there is no need to be worried because you think to yourself, "I've got plenty of time, and eleven more months to catch up." Now time goes by, and at the end of March you're still a little bit behind but again you're not too worried because it's only March. You see where I'm going with this? The idea of My Strategic Thinking is that you cannot wait a year to analyze your progress or waiting and hoping for change. By breaking it down into 4 years per one calendar year you will analyze yourself more often. Because, 90 days or 13 weeks from now becomes your year end, therefore fewer days can be wasted. The focus becomes daily and weekly, not monthly and quarterly. So, let's now take a look at the same situation as above, only using strategic thinking.

Instead of your income goal being $100,000 per year, it is now shifted to $25,000 per year. With the proper strategic plan, you will break that down even more, because I know there are 13 weeks in my year now so that means that you need to make roughly $8,300 a month, or just about $2,000 per week. Now, in the evaluation process you will know if you are behind at the end of each day or week and you can fix the problem NOW instead of waiting until the end of the year to see if the plan worked or not. It's almost like having a cut on your skin. You're not going to wait a couple days in hopes it stops bleeding. You are going to figure out how to stop the bleeding as soon as possible. If something is not working it's better to know immediately than to waste time hoping for it to correct itself.

Don't think this program is all about changing from "annual thinking" to "quarterly thinking," you will miss the boat. It is about implementing a system to teach you to write a proper plan. To focus on important money making blue chip activates. It is about creating urgency and focus on a day to day basis.

Understand that greatness happens in the moment, and that today matters. What you do "today" this very moment must align with your ultimate vision and plan. In an annual environment it becomes easy to put off difficult activities and decision making, because you tell yourself you have time. It is not uncommon for people to begin deferring decisions to the next calendar year because they ran out of time. When operating in annualized thinking, things happen slowly and you will hardly notice when something goes wrong. Eventually you are 3 to 5 years down the road and your business is failing or not profitable and you are wondering why. Why wait that long to find out?

If you're having doubts about what I'm talking about, then think about how productive you are the day or two before you go on a vacation. You will know about a vacation for months. Yet you wait until the final 48 hours to cram in all of your last-minute packing and shopping. Or, look how productive you or your company is just before year end. In most cases you have more energy and you work at a higher pace to get things done before you leave or your timeframe is up, and move from task to task very quickly. You don't waste any time.

Insurance companies experience this increase in sales and productivity twice a year. Once in in January when every sales agent in the company has this "New Year" push, and then in June, which is most year ends for the industry because all the agents are trying to qualify to make council (which are the awards for top producers, which comes with trips and bonuses). The bigger question is why these two months? The answer is deadlines and focus.

So, what if we could create those deadlines and focus every 12 or 13 weeks? Every month or week? What is the potential? Just imagine being that productive every day, may be scary. However, you need to realize the opportunity you create for yourself when you can be that productive all of the time!

The reality is that every month, every week, every day, every hour is crucial to your overall plan. Be conscious of the importance of your daily execution, and don't put off the blue chip meeting until tomorrow. In order to perform at your best, you need to shy away from annualized thinking, and move into short term thinking. Life happens now, and what you do today is creating a result that you cannot see yet.

People have asked me what it takes to run a multi-million-dollar company? What does it take to run a billion-dollar company? The response I give them is; different levels of thinking, planning, and execution. When you run a small private business or you are a one man or woman show, the decisions and thinking you implement is on an immediate basis. If you make a change to something today it will happen tomorrow. It is like driving a speed boat. When you turn, it will be quick and precise. When you make a change in a large company or make a decision in some way, it will take up to 6 months before any results are noticed. So, thinking changes, because decisions you are making today will not impact your tomorrow, tomorrows results will be based on decisions made months prior.

Running large organizations are like driving cruise ships. When I order the ship to turn, it will be a slow wide turn that takes time. When I have spoken to CEOs who run very large companies, they have enlightened me that decisions and visions are targeted approximately 5 years down the road. They are anticipating law changes, product changes, technology changes, and value of the dollar. Decisions are being made today that the public may not see for another 5-10 years. That is why CEOs of Ford and Apple, Microsoft, or Movie directors get paid what they do. Not many people on this planet can even think on that level.

Think about Steve Jobs when he created the IPod and IPhone, or James Cameron when Making Avatar, it took him 10 years! Because his 3D technology didn't even exist at the time, and he waited in the anticipation that it would happen. The goal is that systems will run your business, systems properly implemented will take you to new levels and will allow breakthrough.

# -A Deadline is a Terrific

# Motivator-

"Come in and check us out, yearend prices SLASHED in half, come get your new car today 0% interest for qualified buyers!" does anything like this sound familiar? Ever notice that a lot of companies advertise at year end to boost sales, and it seems they are all giving away the products cheap? Well, the fact is that it works. At the end of the year all companies, sales representatives, etc. typically have some sort of record breaking months and achieve much higher rates of sales because everyone is in a crunch to hit their annualized goals. It has taken them a full year to realize they were behind. So, they are all in a last chance mode to catch up. This is known as the year-end push. The difference between achieving what you set out to do for the year can hang in the balance in those final months.

In the insurance industry, all of the years I have been in the business, and all of the companies I have helped consult with, it seems that 30 to 40 percent of the company's sales spike in the 4th quarter. The reason for this is because of awards, free trips, and bonuses that companies entice with if goals are reached. Once you learn to step away from annualized thinking you will be able to do this every month and always be producing at high numbers. The real benefit is the confidence and peace in knowing you are ahead of where you want to be.

What I coach people to do on our plan is take 12 weeks in place of your 12 months. If you hit your goals in the 12 weeks and follow your plan, then that 13th week is reserved for rewards, and a vacation week. This will preserve the fight people have to work toward something. If you are short of your goals then there is no award or trip, and you get back to your strategic plan and evaluate why you fell short and tweak what needs to be fixed.

What is so powerful about this program is when it is implemented in your personal life or business, you become a person who is always organized and people will follow your lead.

The term "periodization" which is what my program is built after, is the attempt to categorize or divide time into named blocks that are descriptive and measurable. I was told that it began in athletic training and was a technique used to enhance performance. When I was playing football in school, our coach had his periodization system down to the minute and all of the players knew how to follow the plan. For example, we all knew Mondays were:

- o 3:00 PM- Meetings
- o 3:30 PM- Video/Scouting
- o 4:15 PM- Track
- o 5:00 PM- Offense

Every day it was broken down for different events. It was strictly followed down to the exact minute. If we were not able to finish a particular play we were learning, it was ok because we knew that Wednesday at 5:15 PM during our next offensive block we would finish it then. As a result of following our strategic plan, everything that was important was accomplished and resulted in us winning championships and breaking records. On the other hand, I have played for coaches who just coach what comes to their mind during that moment. However, the results are things being forgotten to get done, overall hurting the team, and could never control progress. This is the same in the business world.

If you take your daily routine and just do what comes across your desk, you will go home at the end of the day with 100 things left to do and thinking "what did I even accomplish today?" There is a huge difference between being busy and being productive. You can spend 5 hours talking on the phone, driving, checking emails, and taking lunch, or you can spend 5 hours in front of potential clients or customers. Which do you think will reward you more?

At its core, periodization for sports is a focused training regimen that concentrates on one skill at a time for a limited period, usually four to six weeks. After each period of time, the athlete then moves to the next skill in sequence. I have adopted this technique and I use it in my daily routine, because it is a critical factor that has proven to drive production and balance in my life.

Strategic thinking will define what is important for you to do today, so that tomorrow your objectives can become reality. It is important to understand that for every action you take, a result is generated. Now, with that said, every action does not necessarily mean you will get the result you want. But none the less, every action creates a result.

What creates action? The answer is: your thinking. Everything you do in your life, whether business or personal is created twice. First: mentally and then: physically. It is your thinking that creates actions, and it is your actions that produce results. So, if you learn to control your thinking you ultimately control your results. If your thinking is wrong then your execution will not matter. In the long run, your actions are always going to be side by side with your thinking. When you shift your thinking, everything else will change with it. It is when that occurs that you experience break through.

My coaching clinic provides the tools and focus for individuals and organizations of any size to be highly successful through implementing proper strategic thinking. It creates a sense of clarity, confidence, and certainty with regards to what is important and what is not. You must intensify your focus and create energy, eliminate wishful thinking, and confront reality. Always remember to think big, act big, and then you will see big results.

When I entered the financial services industry, I hired a business coach right away, because as I looked around at all of the successful people in the company, they all had one. When I noticed that people who were struggling didn't have one, I decided that was what I needed. When I hired my business coach we talked each Monday night for one hour, sometimes only a half hour. We would discuss everything from business to my personal life. I remember times when I would hang up the phone and wonder why in the world I was paying this guy a monthly fee to talk. Sometimes I can honestly say I got nothing out of our call, but there were those days I call magical. When he would say something, or give me an idea or critique, which would make that light bulb go off. That one simple idea would end up making me thousands of dollars.

I quickly realized why the best are the best. They listen and never stop leaning. They enroll in coaching programs, read books that pertain to their business, and network. All it takes is just one idea, one spark that will ignite your mind. I have never met someone who has become real successful when they only have themselves to mirror after. You need to be coached, and encouraged in order to be fed ideas. A coach will help when you stumble, or get caught in the valley of despair. Don't look at the cost of a coach as a negative; it is a very important investment in your future.

When I was younger my dad asked me what my dreams in life were. After I told him, he said,

> "Tony, if your dreams are to jump and land on the moon, I want you to know that one of two things will happen. One; you will do all and everything you can do, work very hard, and you will land on the moon. Or two; you will do all and everything you can you can do, work very hard, but you will jump and only make it half way there. That's just life…so I want your dreams to be to jump and land on the stars, because one of two things will happen. One; you will do all and everything you can do, work very hard, and you will land on the stars. Or two; you will do all and everything you can do, work very hard, but you will jump and land half way…on the moon. This is where you wanted to be anyway."

A lot of people never hit their goals. Just think of New Year's resolutions, "I want to lose weight" or "I want to quit smoking." Whatever it is, reality is most people fall short and it's not because they don't have the ability to. It's because the set goals they "intend" to do verse being "committed" to do. Most people never allow themselves to dream big enough.

# -Critical Objectives-

Failure comes only when we forget our ideals, objectives, and principles. Critical objectives are emotional underpinnings that propel us forward through difficulties and uncertainty. In order to execute a plan to its full potential, we must all have critical objectives for doing the things that we do. Otherwise, there would not be a reason to do it. Have you ever thought about why you get out of bed in the morning? Unfortunately, most people abandon a task because of the short-term cost that are involved. People feel that it outweighs the long-term benefits. I have found that if you sit down and create your plan and goals with an emotional stake tied to the outcome of each of them, you will have a higher rate of execution than you would otherwise.

But how do you create a powerful emotion to attach to a goal? First, you must clarify and connect what is important in your life, to your goal. For example, let's assume your income goal is

$100,000. Your attached emotion to this goal may be the fact that, if you don't make that income your family will be forced to move out of the home. Being the sole provider of the home, you will do everything in your power to not see your family hurt like that and nothing will get in your way.

That is an example of emotion that is attached to the outcome of the goals, and is no longer something that you "just do." This connection is ultimately what creates the strength and determination necessary to work through the difficult tasks and fight through the valley of despair. Think about what you truly want for yourself, or for your family. What legacy do you want to create and be remembered for? Think about what you want to do with the time you have been given on this earth.

Everything we do, as much as we try to separate business and personal life, are all connected. When your personal life is in disarray, or your business is failing, it will affect you mentally. Which will create a result, that is most likely is negative in other aspects of your life. That is why it is important to merge the two together in your planning process.

Most of you have experience with creating vision statements. Think of a time when you and your company or partners, got together for a day or two and created a mission statement that was very specific and all of you spent hours figuring out what should be included. Finally, after hours of working on the wording, the group deliberates and agrees that it's perfect. Next, you put someone in charge of promoting the statement, framing it, hanging it in your conference room, and adding it to the website where it will sit. At which point the vision or mission statement was all but forgotten, until a few years later when it comes time to re-write the statement. The greats of this world not only create the vision in their minds, and on paper, but they literally become what they say they wanted. Remember that it is not what you do that is important; it is who you are being.

However, this is not what I am talking about when I say to create critical objectives and statements. If you are going to perform at an expert level you need to take new ground. If you want to be great or make money you must first become great and create money mentally.

You need vision that will allow you to perform at a level greater than you have ever done before and it must be much bigger than the present; one that can be emotionally connected with. Without a compelling vision which is connected to you mentally, you will find that there is no reason to go through the pain of change in order to reach higher levels.

Vision is the starting point to any creation, and definitely the starting point of high performance. The biggest barrier in performance is mental creation. You must believe you can jump out of the jar as the fleas couldn't. You must believe mentally that you can get over that mountain as the little engine that could did.

So, to start on creating that vision you first need to be very clear on what it is that you want to create. For most people, they focus on the business side of life when creating a vision. However, business is only a small part of life, and it is your personal life that should be connected with your business vision because they will go hand in hand.

So, let's start by creating a personal vision. What do you want your life to look like in 3 years from today? Use that to start your business vision. Think about why it is important. You cannot be self-employed and expect to have all of the free time in the world to travel with your kids and wife, if your business requires you to be in it. So, if your personal vision to start is: to spend 3 hours a day with my kids and take my family on 3 vacations a year, then your business vision must allow that to be possible. In order to tap into that, you need to create a plan that is bigger than your present.

To create breakthrough, you will need to open the door to the next plato of life, navigate through fear and discomfort. Life is cyclical, and as such you need to expect that it is going to give back everything that you give it. If you want more competence in your staff, improve your competence etc. If you lack passion in either your business or personal life, figure out how to fix that first. When creating a critical objective for your strategic plan, establish a very specific and time bound personal goal that has emotional resonance. Next, create the emotional link to your business. Once you understand that link, you can define exactly what level of income or production your business can deliver, in order to support your personal thought.

# -Developing Your Strategic Plan-

P lanning is bringing the future into the present, so that you can do something about it now. After you work to determine your visions, both personally and for your business, the next step is to begin designing your strategic plan. A strategic plan is going to be the navigation system you will use to get you where you want to be; which is bringing your dreams and visions to reality. The more direct and specific that you make the plan, the better you will be.

Imagine trying to drive across the country with very general directions and a few road names. You have a higher probability of getting lost as opposed to turn by turn, voice navigation. Having a detailed plan to achieve your vision is even more essential than having that map. Yet the unfortunate thing is that the majority of people will spend more time planning a trip to Disney World, than they will planning for their business.

Planning allows you to think about what you're doing in advance, and allows you the ability to approach your goals with confidence. If you make a mistake on paper you are still ok. However, if you make a mistake in the real world someone will get hurt.

Studies have shown that planning saves significant time and resources. This may seem paradoxical; in fact, many people feel that if they are not constantly doing something, they are not being productive. The reality is that planning your time is more important than planning tasks. When was the last time you blocked off time on your calendar just for planning? Here is a look at my calendar every single week before I add in tasks and appointments (see below).

| | 27 Monday | 28 Tuesday | 29 Wednesday | 30 Thursday | 1 Friday |
|---|---|---|---|---|---|
| 8 am | 6-9 AM Stratigic Block | | 7-4 pm Open Apts. | Buffer Block | 8-10 am Open Apts. |
| 9 00 | | Buffer Block | | 9-5 pm Open Apts. | |
| 10 00 | WAM | 10-5pm Open Apts. | | | |
| 11 00 | | | | | Buffer Block |
| 12 pm | | | | | Break-out Block |
| 1 00 | | | | | |
| 2 00 | Buffer Block | | | | |
| 3 00 | Open Apts. | | | | |
| 4 00 | | | Buffer Block | | |
| 5 00 | | | | | |

Having a set calendar allows you a specific routine, as well as, allows everyone in your company to know when it's ok to come in your office, and allows your assistant to know your availability for appointments.

Strategic planning is on a 13-week basis; however, we schedule work for 12 weeks. This is very different than any other type of planning because, every week is important and all of the tasks on a daily basis need to be "blue chip" tasks. Every 12 to 13 weeks is a new year, a new start and a fresh opportunity. Keep this in mind also when it comes to hiring someone. Let them know how your company operates on periodization. Instead of allowing someone months to a year to prove themselves, they only get 13 weeks, because that is a year to your company.

12-week planning allows you to be more predictable. When you plan further into the future the less certainty you have, because who knows what life will throw at you in the meantime. Short term 12-13 week planning is more focused. What I have found over the years, is that most plans are too scattered and important things that need to get done get pushed further into the future, which is why a lot of plans fail to be executed on time. So, in order to focus on the "blue chip" tasks and strategies, you will need to determine what is going to have the greatest impact in that 13-week period of time. Next, is structure.

Most plans are written with the unspoken goal of developing a good plan. They are then placed in a nice binder and laid to rest on your desk. In which you might glance at from time to time. The entire point of planning is to identify what needs to get done, in order to accomplish a goal. You need to determine; who, what, how. Those three things are crucial when developing a plan. You start with a period goal. A period goal is your overall goal for your 12 - 13 week year. This needs to be very specific and measurable, so at the end of your year you can determine if it was accomplished. Next, we dive deeper, because in order to achieve your period goal you will need strategies for how to achieve the goal.

We can all come up with many, many strategies. However, to be focused, only choose the three best strategies. If you accomplish the strategies then your goal should be accomplished too. Again, make it as detailed and measurable as possible so that, if your period goal is not accomplished, you can change the 1 or 3 strategies that did not work and figure out why.

Finally, we go into even more focus and detail by creating tasks to accomplish the strategies. These will be your day to day activities that are your job. If you finish all of the tasks then you should accomplish your strategy and in the end accomplish the period goal, "if you take care of the minutes, the days take care of itself." Literally make the tasks so easy and specific that anyone should understand it. The goal is different depending on your job and you may need to delegate tasks to others. Usually you will want 15-30 tasks per strategy.

Example: Life Insurance Agent

## Period Goal

- Create and implement a system that will generate $25,000 of realized income by period end (month/year).

## Strategy #1

- Market and hold one sales seminar per week, with minimum 25 guests at each event, which generates minimum $2,000 per event.

## Strategy #2

- Set up referral system that generates 5 new referrals per week. That result in minimum 1 sale per week.

## Strategy #3

- Meet with 10 people per week, 5 of those 10 being 1st time appointments which leads to minimum 4 sales per week generating minimum $2,000 in commission.

The tactics you will create for each strategy will dive into the HOW to accomplish each of the three. Be very detailed and descriptive because these are your day to day activates.

In my program, our clients who use this are emailed every Monday morning at 5:00 AM their list of tactics for the week and on what days to complete them on. If you are doing this on your own, you will need to do the same. Here is an example for strategy #1 above.

Monday:

1. Get online and search for seminar marketing companies
2. Get online and search for restaurants or hotels to hold the seminar
3. Prepare script for seminar
4. Create list and shop for seminar materials

Tuesday:

1. Call (name of seminar company) to get price quote and set up event
2. Call (restaurant or hotel) to confirm date and time of event
3. Browse and determine marketing ideas
4. Study script and presentation
5. Purchase marketing list (age 50+, income or investable, assets of $200,000+ 30miles radius)

Wednesday:

1. Call and pay for radio advertisement
2. Draw, and finalize billboard advertisement
3. Pay and mail, mass mailing invitation
4. Send mass e-mail blitz to potential guests

Thursday:

1. Call and confirm restaurant or hotel

2. Call and confirm each registered guest

3. Study seminar presentation live at event

Anyway, you get the idea. These are your "blue chip" tasks that need to get done no matter what else comes across your desk that week. Make sure your plan is powerful, a realistic stretch and measurable. 12 weeks is long enough to accomplish any goal yet short enough to create and maintain a sense of urgency. While eliminating confusion and delays, you will then operate as a top performer.

# -Power of the Moment-

What you see today in your life is the result of something you did in your past. The actions that you take every day in your job, right now, even reading this book, will create a result for tomorrow. Michael Jordan said, "I've missed more than 9,000 shots in my career. I've lost almost 300 games; 26 times I've been trusted with the game winning shot and missed." It was discovered that while you plan for your future, you still act in the day. To be truly effective, our daily activity must align with our long-term vision, strategy, and tactics.

Even though Michael Jordan missed many shots, as we will miss many business opportunities, his success on the court was a direct result of the hours a day he practiced his shots and practiced perfection. His day to day routine sculpted him into the hall of fame athlete he is today.

When I was little, my dad always used to say, "practice doesn't make perfect." And I would get this confused look on my face, because that's not what everyone else says. Then he would go on to finish saying "prefect practice, make perfect, because if you practice the incorrect way you will fail." It is ok to miss and fail or "climb to failure" (we will discuss that later in the section) because that is how we learn, and achieve success as we continue in life.

However, without planning for the moment, you will not set up tomorrow the way you want it. Your weekly tasks become powerful, because those are your weekly "game plans" as athletes and coaches use the week before a game. Please note that these weekly plans are not a "to-do" list. It is the reflection of the critical strategy from the 13-week plan that needs to take place in the current week in order to breakthrough. It is more or less a derivative or your period plan, it is 1/13$^{th}$ the slice of your 13-week year.

Now, every morning before you start your workday, I recommend using 5 minutes to plan your day. This extra 40 minutes per week can improve your effectiveness by 300%, which has been measured! By focusing your attention, this is the first step of many in becoming great versus mediocre.

To really take full advantage of this plan, I recommend printing it out and hold it in your hand, and use it throughout the day. Check things off as you do them, so you can stay on top of your progress. I know most of you have IPhones and IPads, but physical paper will keep your attention to the tasks at hand. It will become your personal assistant, when you ask yourself "what's next?" All you have to do is look down. When it comes time to go home for the night, and you have a task left that was not checked off, you failed the day, and it allows you to know immediately when you fall behind on the plan. This is important because it guides you through execution, and ensures you accomplish the days so that the weeks take care of themselves.

# -Keeping Score-

I am a big sports fanatic, and so are many millions of people in the world today. Have you ever wondered why sports are so motivating, not only to watch but to play? Because there is a competition involved! Two teams battling for one thing: to win. The art of the sport is rewarded and tracked by the score of the game. Champions are determined by the score of the game. Can you imagine people spectating as you work and did your job? Or paying for the privilege to see you in action? Keeping track of the score of a sporting event is really the heart of the competition, and of course if sports betting is involved it is the only thing that matters.

The score is a measurement of that team's success and hard work. My question to you is; do you think Michael Jordan became great when he won his 6th NBA championship? The response I hear most is: absolutely! However, my answer would be no. Michael Jordan became great when he was a little boy practicing, playing basketball with his father in their back yard. Remember practice doesn't make perfect, perfect practice makes perfect. And he would stay out all night until he accomplished what he wanted. Great athletes and enterprises are built today; the championship, victory, or the promotion is just the result of the actions being taken in the past.

You can use scorekeeping as a measurement for success and also to identify areas of improvement. At any point during a game, the players, coaches, and spectators know exactly where that team stands overall and also where they need improvement in order to better their score. If nobody was watching or keeping score, no one would never know how or what to fix. How interesting would sports be if they didn't keep score or individual stats?

This information provides a base knowledge which allows a person or management to make decisions that can alter the outcome of the situation. In other words, scorekeeping lets us know if what we are doing is effective.

Not a lot of companies in the business world keep score, and that may very well be the reason for most down falls. Without keeping score, without some objective measure, we cannot know for certain if what we are doing is correct. Just as keeping score motivates players on an emotional level, the same applies in the work atmosphere.

In the 1960s Frederick Herzberg, an industrial psychologist, set out to determine what motivates people in the workplace. His extensive research identified the top two motivators as: 1. Achievements, and 2. Recognition. I contend that the only way to know if you are achieving is through measurement. Yet a common misconception is that scoring damages self-esteem. Research however, indicates the opposite, that measurement builds self-esteem and confidence. Measurement is a reality check that provides performance feedback. It will remove the emotion and paint an honest picture of your performance. We all love to win and hate to lose, we all aim to pleas and not want to disappoint.

Charles Schwab had a mill manager whose people were not producing their quota of work. "How is it," Schwab asked him, "that a manager as capable as you, can't make this mill turn out what is should?" "I don't know," the manager replied. "I've sworn and cursed and I've threatened them with demotion or being fired. But nothing is working, they are just lazy." This conversation took place at the end of the day, just before the night shift came on. Charles Schwab asked the manager for a piece of chalk, then, turning to the nearest man, asked, "How many heats did your shift make today?" "Six." Without another word, Schwab chalked a big figure SIX on the floor, and walked away.

When the night shift came in, they saw the "6" and asked what it meant. "The big boss was in here today," the day shift said. "He asked us how many heats we did, and we told him six, so he chalked it on the floor and left." The next morning Schwab walked through the mill again. The night shift had rubbed out the "6" and replaced it with a big "7". When the day shift reported for work the next morning, they saw the "7" on the floor. The night shift through they were better did they? Well, they would show them a thing or two. The crew pitched in with enthusiasm, and when they quit that night, they left behind an enormous, swaggering "10".

Things were rapidly picking up pace at the mill, the same mill that was lagging in production, was now out performing all the other mills around. Simple, quick, cheap, and powerful, Schwab's improvised "leader-board" literally gave the mill workers something to look up to. You see, we all have a tendency from time to time, to rationalize lackluster results.

When keeping score, we are forced to confront the reality of our situation and, if appropriate, our lack of results. The good part is that when forced to confront reality it wakes us up, and the sooner our actions can be put towards producing results.

Measurement drives the execution process. If you are a sales person or working by yourself it would be a good idea to keep score of your personal performance. I am not talking about scoring the overall company as a whole that can be done by stock price. I am talking about your personal execution. You should know if YOU are profitable or not. Know if what you are doing on a daily basis is helping or hurting you.

For example, if you are a sales representative for an insurance company; is checking your email helping you sell life insurance? Is taking that extra hour for lunch helping you get new leads? Score keeping your day to day activities is a very important part of strategic thinking, because everything should be done for a reason.

Measurement allows you to provide important data to yourself or for your employees, which in return will allow you to make intelligent decisions. It will combine both lead and lag indicators that provide comprehensive feedback that is necessary for informed decision making. Just to be clear, lag indicators are the end results that you are striving to achieve. Things like; income, sales, commissions, and relationships. Lead indicators are the activities that produce the end results (lead = actions, Lag = results). Most companies and individuals effectively measures lag indicators, but many fail to develop score keeping for lead indicators.

For example, if you were to spend $5,000 on a seminar to bring people to the event, most people would just track the outcome of the seminar in terms of sales or dollars put back in your pocket. But why not keep score of the marketing and the amount of people who show up from certain areas versus the amount of mailers sent out. What was your response rate? Why not track the presenter's ability to effectively get people to sign up for the program? Can that presenter close 10% of the people in the room or 60% of the people in the room? You need to know, what areas are higher response, what speakers are best at articulating the presentation, track what information people are interested in hearing, etc. Do not just show up and say, "Hey I made $6,000 in sales today" and think that will work every time you put on a show, because it won't and you need to know why. Every part of the lead indicator process must be recorded.

Think of science, if you are trying to find a solution to a problem, you have to measure one variable at a time. If there is more than one variable bring measured at a time, then the solution cannot be fully evaluated. Therefore, every single aspect must be measured individually, so the results can be tracked. Over 60% of the time, breakdown occurs in the execution process, but most people assume the plan is at fault, so they change the plan. Effective measurement will help you pinpoint the breakdown, so that you can address it head on.

Let's go back to my example of the seminar. Let's say your goal is to get 30 sales this period and you expect 10 to come from seminars, 10 to come from cold calling, and 10 to come from email marketing. At the end of the period, you see that you only have 20 sales completed. Most people will say the plan didn't work; the tactics I implemented were ineffective. By proper score keeping you will be able to go back and analyze, that the seminars worked to perfection, you got all 10 sales. However, the cold calling yielded you 5 sales as well as the email marketing. Now, to me it's not necessarily that the plan didn't work. Maybe, your execution of cold calling was ineffective.

There are many variables to cold calling that need to be tracked, so you can tell if that was the problem or not. Such as: did you call 100 people per day like the plan said, or did you only call

92 people and say it was close enough. Is your script or phone presentation up to par or did you sound like a robot etc. Without knowing EXACTLY where the mistakes were made you cannot fix the solution.

This is why score keeping is so important. My company tracks performance by what I call the "weekly score card." It allows you to grade your weekly performance every Friday evening, based on the individual tactics that your plan says needs to be done that particular week. For example:

<u>Weekly Score Card</u>

☑ Speak to 10 people, and ask for a sale       10/10

☐ $2,000 realized income       1,500/2,000

☐ 1000 Calls during the week       900/1,000

☑ 10 new referrals       10/10

☑ 10,000 emails blitz       <u>10,000/10,000</u>

(Use our system or calculator to determine %)       95%/100%

I urge you to strive for excellence not perfection. I have found that if you maintain 80% or better each week you will always achieve your objectives. If I notice that you are doing 100% every week, for all you "A" students out there, I want you to know I view that as a bad thing. Because to me that only means your plans are too easy, or you're not doing it correctly. If first you succeed, next time try something harder.

Measurement drives the process, effective measurement is essential for top performers, and makes sure it includes lead and lag indicators. If you are the boss or a manager, during your Monday morning WAM (weekly accountability meeting) gather all of the employees in the room and make everyone read their weekly scores out loud. It is easy for someone to make up an excuse one-on-one for why they scored a 40%, but in front of everyone they won't like that. So, it makes them work harder to spare the embarrassment.

# -Do Everything Intentionally-

A young boy in school was asked by his coach when he will be ready to play again after an injury that occurred in practice the week prior. The boy replied, "The doctor told me it will take time to heal, probably a week or two." The coach nodded his head and went on with his day. A few weeks later the coach returned to the boy and again asked if he was ready to return to the field. The boy said, "Yes, I am all healed up, but I was unable to work out and it will take time to get my strength back." The coach nodded his head and went on with his day. The boy a few weeks later went to his coach and told him he was finally ready to get back to the game. This time the coach replied, "Sorry kid, too much time has passed and we found a replacement for your position. In time, you will have the opportunity to compete for the spot." The boy saddened went on with his day.

Many years later the boy was now in college and was told he had an exam in the upcoming month. As most boys do, he told himself I have plenty of time to study for this test, and went out with his friends. Weeks passed and the boy was finally confronted with the reality that the test was tomorrow. He stayed up all night studying for this test. As the next day came, he realized he was not ready and needed more time; as a result, he failed his test.

As his life went by, he learned time was important and began to focus his intentions on time management, working very hard and achieving his business dreams. The boy was now an old man who only had a little time left. At home that night he sat down and reflected on his life. He realized that when he was young he never planned for time. In his middle years, he did plan for time management and accomplished everything he strived for. However, in old age the man realized he failed to plan for time with his family, and now he had run out of time.

In the end, we have more control of our actions than we do our outcomes. Ultimately our results are created by our actions. It stands to reason then, that the actions we choose to engage in throughout our day ultimately determine our destiny. Yet too often people engage the day on its own terms. In other words, they perform the various day to day white chips that pop up randomly.

Planning for time is important, but you must plan for everything. To take your performance in life, both in business and personally, you need to be more intentional about your use of time.

Intentionality is the opposite of reactive. It requires you to reorganize yourself around what you choose to be a priority, which aligns with your goals and vision. When you become intentional, you become aware when you are procrastinating or engaging in low level activates. "If we take care of the minutes, the years will take care of themselves." The challenge we all face is planning to far in the future.

You hear athletes saying at the beginning of the year their goal is to win the championship. Instead of saying their goal is to win the 1st game. When you plan to far in advance your mind is also living in the future, resulting in days flying by like in the story above with the boy. If you simply take care of right now, or just go win this week's game, the championship will happen on its own.

The key to successful use of time is intentional use of time. Not necessarily trying to eliminate these unplanned interruptions, but to schedule time to focus on strategically important items first.

Performance time is a system I have that utilizes time blocking to take back control of your day and maximize your effectiveness. Here are three main parts of time performance, and then I will show you what my calendar looks like before every week.

1. STRATEGIC BLOCK: a strategic block is a 3-hour block of uninterrupted time that is scheduled in advance. During these blocks, you DO NOT accept phone calls, faxes, emails, or visitors. You do not do anything other than work

on the blue chip tasks of your strategic plan. Your entire money-making activities. Doing this allows you a guarantee that these tasks will get done, without realizing at the end of the week that you forgot. You will be amazed by the quantity and quality of work you will produce in this block of time.

2.  BUFFER BLOCK: a buffer block is time that is created to deal with all of the unplanned and low-level activities that arise throughout the day. Nothing is more unproductive and frustrating than having to deal with constant interruptions during the day. Yet we all have days where unplanned issues dominate our work day. This time should be set in advance to handle voicemails, walk-ins, emails etc. It should be 30-60 minutes per day that people know is the time to get a hold of you if they need to.

3.  BREAK-OUT BLOCK: one of the key factors contributing to performance plateaus is the absence of time. Entrepreneurs and people in general get caught up working longer and harder, and end up sacrificing personal time for themselves. You see a person go into work all day, come home to be with family, put the kids to bed, spend an hour or so with the spouse, go to bed, and do it all over again the next day. This creates a large amount of stress on the individual. Break-out blocks are good source of energy and enthusiasm builder. This block of time should be a 3-hour

block of time that takes you away from the business during normal business hours. This time is designated to refresh and reinvigorate, so when you return to work you are again ready to effectively focus. The time block can and should be used for EVERYTHING that you do from when you will eat lunch, when you answer phones, when you leave the office, when you have a meeting, and when to pick up the phone to dial out to a client. It can and should be as detailed as possible. Even as far as blocking date nights with drive time.

For many of the clients I have worked with, the more detailed you are about time, the greater impact it had on performance. Learn to be intentional with time and you won't runout.

EXAMPLE CALANDER BEFORE WEEK:

| | 27 Monday | 28 Tuesday | 29 Wednesday | 30 Thursday | 1 Friday |
|---|---|---|---|---|---|
| 8 am | 7-10 am Strategic Block | 8-9 am Buffer | Apt. Times | 8-9 am Buffer | 8 am-2 pm Apt. Times |
| 9 00 | | Apt. Times | | Apt. Times | |
| 10 00 | 10-10:30 WAM | | | | |
| 11 00 | 10:30-12 Buffer | | | | |
| 12 pm | 12-1 pm Lunch | | 12-1 pm Lunch | 12:30-1:30 Lunch | |
| 1 00 | 1-5 pm Open Apts. | | 1-2 pm Buffer | 1:30-5 pm Break-out | |
| 2 00 | | | Apt. times | | 2-3 pm Buffer |
| 3 00 | | | | | Off |
| 4 00 | | | | | |
| 5 00 | | | | | |

(Above) see all of my week is blocked out for what I am going to do, and here are specific openings when I will take appointments, so my staff knows when it's ok to schedule. (Below) Next, is an example of how the week may look after my assistant fills the week up.

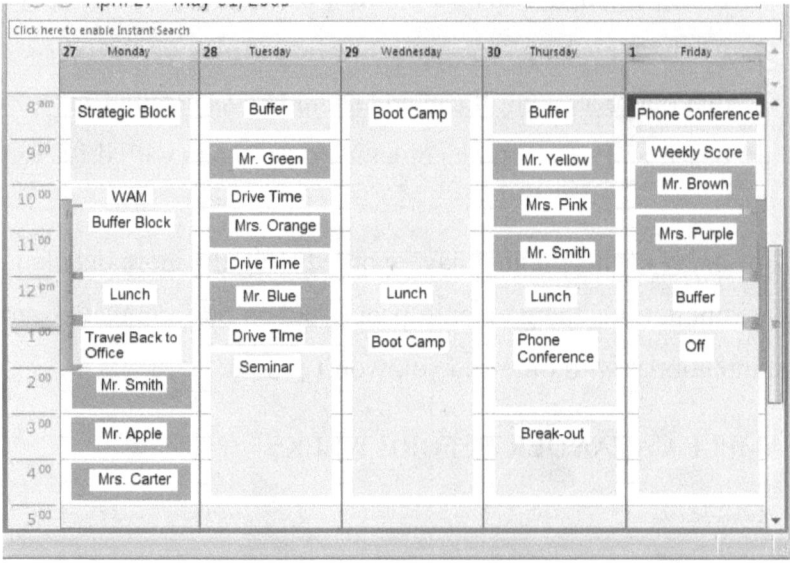

# -Become Accountable-

" Life is not accountable to us, we are accountable to life." Accountability is probably the most misunderstood term used today. The vast majority of people equates accountability with consequence, and as a result, often tries to avoid it.

Whenever you hear the word accountability, you most likely think of someone getting in trouble or wrong doing. Many people try to hold other people accountable and they associate it with bad behavior. No wonder most people want nothing to do with being held accountable.

If you are a manager how many times have you said, "we need to do a better job of holding people accountable?" Or if you are an employee, how many times have you hear that? We mistake accountability for something that can be imposed on an individual, which is not accountability, its consequences.

In fact, if you told someone that you are going to hold them accountable, you are setting yourself up for failure or disappointment, because you cannot "hold" someone accountable. You hold a baby, or a football, but you cannot hold accountability. Being accountable should not be a consequence, it merely is ownership. It is a life trait or willingness to own your actions and results, regardless of the circumstance you find yourself in for you only. Peter Koestenbaum who is an author and philosopher points out that, "we have a small way of thinking about accountability. We believe that it is something that must be to devise reward and punishment schemes to do this. These beliefs are so dominant in our culture today, that they are difficult to question, yet they are the very beliefs that keep us from experiencing what we long for."

The realization that you have choices is being accountable. That in fact there are NO "HAVE-TOs" in life, there are only "CHOOSE-TOs". Some people question me on this issue, but I will stand my ground. Someone says, "I HAVE to pay my house payment." My reply is, "no you do not have to, you simply CHOOSE to." Because if you don't pay it, then you lose your home, so you choose to keep it. When you look at a situation, and tell yourself you "HAVE TO" then it becomes a burden. However, if you approach it and say, "I CHOOSE TO" it becomes your decision. You don't HAVE TO go to the gym; you will just gain weight, so you merely choose to go. You ultimately in every situation have a choice. Don't get the wrong impression that somehow accountability is passive. Quite the opposite, true accountability is very confrontive, but rather than just confronting with consequences, it should be confronted with the freedom of choice, and that the consequence of that choice is your decision. You don't "HAVE TO" show up for work, but if you "CHOOSE" not to, the consequence may be termination.

How you choose to view accountability will affect everything that you do in your life. When you can understand that true accountability is about choice, and taking ownership of that choice, life changes. You move form resistance to empowerment, form limits to possibilities and from average to great. Always strive to see how the choices and decisions you make in every moment, create the life and results you see in the future.

Accountability is not being a victim, but owning up to the fact that there is a problem and at least part of that problem is always you. We cannot control what happens to us in life by other people, but we can choose how to react to it.

If I am unhappy with my relationship, then I must do something about it. I cannot wait for the other person to do it. If I am unhappy with my job, income, or anything else, accountability is about taking ownership of the problem and not playing the victim role.

# -Commitments-

There is a difference between interests and commitments. When you are interested in doing something, you do it only when circumstances permit. When you're committed to something, you accept no excuses, only results. Commitments are powerful; commitments can be the key that opens every door to your future. It becomes a habit. Think back to a time when you really wanted something, and you were absolutely determined to get it no matter how many people said no, and you didn't stop until it was yours. Commitments are an unstoppable force if you are truly committed.

I remember when I was younger and playing football, I was so committed to becoming the best, that I lived every day thinking and studying football. School was second to me, and so were many other things. But I had to sacrifice those things in order to get something I really wanted, which was ultimately to be remembered on the field after my time was done.

A commitment is a personal promise that you make with yourself. Keeping a promise to others, builds trust and respect. However, keeping a promise to yourself builds character, self-esteem, and success. In fact, Webster's dictionary defines commitment as: "the state of being bound emotionally or intellectually to some course of action." A commitment is a conscious decision to take specific action or non-action, to create a desired result. Think of January 1$^{st}$ when everyone rushes to a gym or health club to get their new year's resolutions. They make a promise to themselves to lose 10 Ibs, and then one month later the membership key is sitting on your counter collecting dust. They know if they went 3x a week, they could lose the 10 Ibs, yet they don't. Meanwhile the people who did keep to their commitments are in the best shape ever. It is the same in the business world; the successful people every year have built their character to a point that they are unstoppable, while the rest of the people sit back and wonder why they are not there. When you commit the question of "if" goes away and "how" is put in its place.

Here are some keys to successful commitments:

STRONG DESIRE: In order to fully commit to something, you will need a clear and personally compelling reason. Without a strong desire, you will struggle on the days where implementing becomes difficult. The end result that you are striving to achieve needs to be meaningful enough to get you through hard times and keep you on track.

CLEAR ACTIONS: Once you have an intense desire to accomplish something, you then need to identify the core actions that will produce the result that you are after. In today's world, most of us sit around and watch others because many people are scared to get their hands dirty. Remember, what counts is, what you are doing, you are doing for a cause. It is critical that you identify the one or two core reasons and focus on those actions.

COUNT THE COSTS: In order to make a commitment, you must be aware and come to terms with the effect it will have on you beforehand. For example, if your New Year's resolution is to lose 10 lbs the costs that are involved will be less time with friends, less free time to lay around, and sacrificing many of the current foods you love. If you can prepare for that and you are ok with those costs, then you will be all set. Literally write out a list of pros and cons and acknowledge the obstacles that will be in your way. When the time comes (and it will) when you are in the middle of a situation that involves breaking one of those costs, such as a birthday party with pizza and cake, you will be able to recognize the obstacle and you can decide to pass, because your committed to your plan. Trust me in the end it will be worth it. Plus, by being willful your friends and family will notice and may even follow your lead.

Finally, act on commitments and not feelings. There will be times that you will not feel like doing anything. Maybe a long day after work or just a bad day in general, and you don't feel like going to the gym. It is during times like this that you will need to learn to act on your commitments and not your feelings. If you don't, you are breaking the momentum and when break a promise to yourself you will notice it is much easier to break promises all together. Many times, commitments are made more arduous by the time frame in which they are made. If you say, "I'm going to work out 3x a day all year long" you are more likely to fail on that plan (also notice that was an annual thinking commitment). But, if you make a 12-week commitment to work out 5x per week for 45 minutes, starting January 1st, by the time your 12 weeks year is over, you will have your summer body ready just in time and you are committing the workout for a shorter time frame, raising the probability of success. Commitments are like strategic plans, if you think too far in advance, you will lose sight of the plan.

*"Carpe Diem, seize the day.... Carpe Diem, seize the day boys...make your lives extraordinary."*

*-Robin Williams.*

# -Carpe Diem-

When does a champion become great? The answer I hear most is, when that champion reaches the pinnacle of his career, and is rewarded for his work. When Michael Jordan won his 6th NBA Championship, or when Martin Scorsese won the lifetime achievement award. However, I believe greatness happens the mere instant.... that split second, that person decided to do whatever it took to be that athlete, that writer, or that business person. The results are not the attainment of greatness; results are simply the confirmation to the rest of the world. You become great long before the results show it.

What I find profound is that the difference between mediocre and greatness on a daily and weekly basis is slim, but the difference in the result six months to a year down the road is huge.

The difference between average and great may be two to three extra client meetings a week, or an extra five to ten phone calls a day. It could be 3 hours of a 45-hour work week focusing on a strategic plan and time management. For athletes, the average between being forgotten in history to being remembered in all history books is tenths of seconds, or one point. Who raced against Michael Johnson in the Olympics the year he took the gold with those amazing gold shoes? The answer is, Michael March, and he lost by less than three tenths of a second! In racing Indy cars or NASCAR, the race can be lost by literally inches on a photo finish. In the Super-bowl XXXIV, the Rams were playing the Titans. The Titans drove the ball down with 6 seconds on the clock, and were stopped 1 yard away… 12 inches from a Super-bowl victory.

Each and every one of us has the God given ability to be great. What makes a champion is the discipline to do the extra things even when you don't feel like it. The encouraging news is that regardless of how you have performed in the past or how you are currently performing, you can change by simply choosing to change. "The reality of your life is your actions working their way back to you. Change you actions and you change your reality."

CLIMB TO FALLURE, NOT FAILURE, here is another story for you; this is how to succeed without reaching the top:

(14) My friend Matt and I walked around the bend in the trail, and I stopped dead in my tracks and looked at a beautiful sheet of rock smooth and slightly overhanging, with a thin, fingertip-sized

seam splitting the middle of the silver granite wall. "You can see why I named the route Crystal Ball." Matt said, pointing to a baseball-sized quartzite handhold 50 ft. up.

We roped up and I set off climbing up the route, shooting for an "on-sight" ascent (an on-sight ascent means that on your first try, you lead the climb without prior information about the moves, and without an artificial aid. Other climbers have not told you how to climb the difficult sections, nor have you watched anyone else attempt the route). You get one chance only at an on-sight climb. Once you start to climb, if you blow it and fall onto the rope, you've lost the chance forever.

Ten feet below the crystal, my feet began to skitter about, slipping off slick pebbles, and I curled my thumb around a little edge, think to myself, "if I can just get a little weight off my fingers..." The adrenaline of the on-sight attempt made me over grip every hold, clamping down as hard as I could, like an overanxious runner who goes out too fast in the first 100 meters of a 400-meter race.

I gathered a bit of composure, while hooking my thumb and resting my fingers, trying to get my breathing to settle down. But my mind chattered away: "If I get it wrong, no way I can reverse...and even if I get it right, I'm not sure I'll have enough power to pull up to the crystal ball...and if I can't get to the crystal ball, there's no way I'll be able to get the rope clipped into the next point of protections...how far would I fall?"

Tick, tick, tick. The clock ran on while I hesitated.

"Okay Matt, here I go."

Right hand to the side pulls. Left foot to the edge.

"OH-OH." Wrong call. I should have gone to the edge with my left hand! I rolled my body to the left, griping for an edge, a pebble, a wrinkle –something, anything- that would allow me to pop my right hand up and move my left onto the side edge. I smooshed my right fingers into a little edge that pointed down and sideways- the wrong direction for a good pull. I now had less than 20% chance of success. If I tried to make the move, I'd almost certainly fall, a drop of 30 feet. Even if I did manage to surge upward, the higher I went without trying to "clip" the next bolt, the bigger the eventual fall (to clip means to get the rope into the carabineer hanging off a protection bolt).

"Off!" I called down to Matt.

"NO!" he yelled back. "You're only three moves from the crystal. You can recover there."

"Off!" I yelled.

And I let go, dropping onto the rope in the nicely controlled fall.

I hung up the rope for about 10 minutes, recovering, and then swung toward the rock, pulled myself back onto the holds, and climbed to the top. But of course, it didn't count. I hadn't done a clean on-sight. And even though later that day, I managed to ascend the route from bottom to top in one shoot- a success by most measures- I had none the less failed. Not failed on the climb, but failed in my mind. When confronted with the moment of commitment, the moment of decision, the moment of go-for-it, well, I let go. I went to failure, not fallure.

Failure and fallure, the difference is subtle, but it is all the difference in the world. In fallure, you still do not get up the route, but you never let go. In fallure, you fall; in failure, you let go. Going to fallure means full commitment, even if the odds of success are less than 20%, 10% or even 5%. You leave nothing in reserve, no mental or physical resource untapped. In fallure, you never give yourself a psychological out: "well, I didn't really give it everything...I might have made it with my best effort."

To the outside observer, failure and fallure look similar (you fly through the air in both cases). But the inner experience of fallure is totally different from that of failure. You will only find your true limit when you go to fallure not failure. Sure, he had less than 20% chance of pulling through to the crystal but, because he let go, he will never know for sure. Perhaps he would have had an extra reserve; perhaps he would have surprised himself and had an extra bit of power to hang on for one more move. Or perhaps the next move would have been easier than it looked. And that's the rub, as with life, you don't know what that next hold looks like. It's the ambiguity- about the holds, the moves, and the ability to climb- that makes 100% commitment so difficult.

Sara Little Turnbull said, "If you don't stretch, you don't know where the edge is." She is the director of the Stanford University Process of Change Laboratory. She built a distinguished career as a design consultant to corporations such as Corning and 3M. The Corporate Design Foundation described Turnbull as "CEO's secret weapon in product design development." She said that some of her best designs came from when she was on the brink of a failed concept, but refused to let go of course, many, indeed most, of her brink of failure designs ended up being failures. But every once in a while, by not letting go she would push herself to a completely different level and something extraordinary would come about. And that is when breakthroughs happen, pushing through the valley of despair.

In researching great companies, I have noticed how the best executives understand this idea. As CEO of Kimberly-Clark, Darwin Smith and a fallure verses failure decision in vaulting his company to greatness. For 100 years, Kimberly-Clark languished in mediocrity, with most of its business in traditional paper mills. Smith realized that the company's best shot at greatness lay in the paper-based consumer goods area, where it had a side business called Kleenex, a brand that had become a category, like Coke or Xerox. Like the general who burned the boats upon landing, leaving no retreat for his soldiers, Smith decided to sell the traditional mills. He even sold the mill in Kimberly, Wisconsin, and threw all the proceeds into the consumer business, going head-to-head with rivals, such as Scott paper and Proctor & Gamble. Wall Street derided him, the business media called the move stupid, and the analysts wrote merciless commentary. But in the end, Smiths decisions paid off, and Kimberly-Clark became the number-one paper-based consumer product company in the world.

I now see life as a series of choices between going to failure or fallure. As in an on-sight attempt in climbing, the next hold in life remains unclear. And that very ambiguity keeps us back from making a fully committed attempt. We fail mentally. We let go. We take a nice, controlled fall, rather than risking a bigger fall.

Whether it is starting a business or publishing a book, fallure rarely means doom and most important, the only way to find your true limits to go to fallure, not failure.

# -Finding Your Own Way-

W e have covered many topics over the course of this book, from belief systems, to evaluating stocks, companies and even taxes. I have showed you how to create a strategic plan, and even though we could go into hundreds of pages in more detail, I feel like it is enough education to get you started in the right direction. My advice for what it's worth is to find a coach. "Wisdom doesn't come with age. Nothing does, except wrinkles. It's true, some wines improve with age. But only if the grapes were good in the first place." Abigail Van Buren. I have a list of individuals, mentors and colleagues that I turn to when I need help, and so do many other successful people. It is important to learn as much as you can to always better yourself. Find people who have bigger companies, or who make more money, or have the things that you don't have, and don't be jealous, just ask them to coach you and show you how.

Why I chose to be a coach. My love of coaching began long before I ever sat behind a desk. In fact, it started on a football field. Through a happy accident I found that I love coaching football almost as much as I loved playing it. There is something extremely satisfying about building an offense and watching it all come together against an opposing defense. My friends and family may tell you stories of me always arguing the other side of the story or being "bossy", even though it's hard for me to argue that, I do it because I'm just used to being the coach. I like to help my coaching clients figure out who they are and help them find a niche. And I like to teach and watch people redefine the way they think about money and investing. My goal is to educate them and give them the tools they need to be successful on their own. For some people, asking for help is the hardest question they will ever ask. But realize that it is a necessary question if you want to grow.

# –Giving Back–

I believe that it is important to give back. I feel that the only way to be truly rich is to help others become rich. But I am not talking about money here. Being rich is much more than a balance in your bank account. Some are rich in knowledge, some are rich in ideas, and others are rich with time. The true measure is what you do with it. Be the person who uses what you have to give back.

Here is how I give back and if you are an individual or own a company, let me talk to you about one of my projects that I am passionate about. I started a charity called "The Bravata Foundation" that is dedicated to replacing the financial losses to families who are the victims of financial crimes. The money that The Bravata Foundation raises goes directly to those families and helps them re-build their lives. These people put their faith into companies who were on the up-and-up and whether it was actual fraud or just a company trying to make it and failed, it was devastating to thousands of people in our country who deserve a break. Your donations are tax-deductible and you can be directly involved with helping a grieving family. We have platforms for investing into the charity and you can read more by visiting www.BRAVATAFOUNDATION.org. You can donate monthly by credit card for $9.99 per month or any other rate in which you choose for 12 Months. Or you can be a member of the foundation by choosing one of three memberships.

The Bravata Foundation will soon be holding annual galas and private functions for members to be united with the families who they have helped. These families need trusted financial advisors, lawyers, accountants, etc. We aim to put trusted professionals together to help these families unite with the best of the best so the second time around they can do it the right way.

Please donate and get involved today.
www.BRAVATAFOUNDATION.org

# Afterward

I originally was not planning on covering these topics in this book. However, since this book may lead you to join The Wealth Creator Clinic, to use our strategic planning software, or to hire us as a personal, business, or sales coach. I wanted to talk a little about our services along with our cherished business branding and, leadership development program, that companies send key employees or individuals choose to join to help retain and attract talent, demand higher salaries, or higher fees. And finally, to learn the real qualities of the leader so that people will want to follow your lead.

The second half of the main book covered our strategic planning program. Our software is designed to keep track of all of that for you. We offer 2-Day live boot camps for individuals or companies, where we create the plans for you, or help you build your own. As well as train you on the program itself. The real benefit to you is our execution coaching program that is a weekly phone session with a consultant going over your weeks score card and talking about personal and business issues to help guide you through your strategic plan. Our main focus is to keep you operating at 80% or higher on your plan.

We will get together 4 times per year for our period planning sessions to work out issues on the plans or the revise them in part if they are too easy for you. Remember we are jumping to the stars not the moon.

I will leave with that on this topic because strategic thinking was already a major part of the main book.

# -Sales and Business Coaching-

In this section, I am going to talk about our services in this category as well as talk about a small preview of the information we cover, as far as, a glance at the mind of a customer to selling techniques to target emotions. And then finish with how I can help business owners grow their companies.

Let's start with a brief covering of the psychology of a sale. No matter if you're selling life insurance, real estate, or gym memberships. Most of these topics will be the same. What is variable is whether or not you need to be patience selling or pitch selling. Here is what I mean by these, patience selling is my terminology for non-pushy salesman. Nobody likes to be sold. When a person feels the pressure of a salesman they immediately go into an objection mode, regardless of it they actually want the item or not.

If you are in life insurance sales for example, your job is to get the customer emotionally involved to make that sale. What I find works best, is a 3-meeting process. Meeting number one is a "greeting meeting", whereas you talk to them about family and their life and goals and ask them to show you their current financials and current investments. You will tell them straight up "even if you want to get going today, I'm not going to allow it." You tell them that you first need to get a grasp of their situation to fully understand what they need. You don't walk into a doctor's office with a head ache and tell the doctor you need aspirin. That doctor must give you an MRI to see if there are other problems at play to be able to diagnose the situation. And then you tell the client, "If you are accepted into this program, I will make a recommendation for you." By telling a customer "if" it pulls the item out of their hands, and people always want what they can't have.

After getting copies of all of their financials you set a meeting time for appointment #2. Even if you have ZERO appointments you give them an option of Tuesday at 10 AM or Thursday at 2 PM. This gives the illusion that you are jammed packed and in high demand. Never let a client tell you when the meeting will be. If they say Monday at 12, you say, "that actually won't work for me, I can do Tuesday at 12, how's that?" also note that meeting two and three should be in your office. A doctor does not come to your home; they must go to the doctor. Meeting number one is an informal meeting where your only job is to get them to like you personally. Now you have them scheduled in your office for meeting number two.

This meeting is your pitch, you have looked at their financials, and you put your sales pitch recommendation for their life insurance and annuity needs. When you are finished you say, "It is my job to tell you what you should do; it's your job to tell me what you want me to do." Give them three options, and tell them to go home review them and make a decision. Again, do not make the sale even if they are ready. Make them wait then, schedule meeting three in your office the next day or day after. Tell them to bring a check and a pen and that you will get everything ready for an approval. This three-step process will get your closing percent higher, develop trust with your client, and get more from your client in short term and long-term sales.

There is way more to these sales techniques but that is what our program is for. This can work for insurance, real estate, lawyers, and really any industry that has to retain a person for a long period of time.

Pitch sales is a totally different ballgame. Quick pitches are for product companies, which may never see a specific individual ever again. Their main focus is only to make a sale now, most of the time impulse. From cars, gym memberships, selling grills at Costco. You don't have time to let them walk away, and you have 10 seconds to get their attention and 60 seconds to sell them. The longer they stay with you the better your closing percent. Your eyes must stay on the product, you talk loudly and point. You place the product in their hands and quickly sell them on why they can't leave without this today.

Pitch sales training is not as easy, however that is what we are here for. It's to help change your mind and teach you how to tap into a "must have" sales mentality.

We again do weekly coaching and discuss case preparation or selling techniques. You have access to dozens of training videos and scripts to watch and learn form to mold into your own process. We take you on a journey to change your style from speech patterns to clothing that will enhance your bottom line. You will learn marketing and branding techniques that will practically make the sale for you. And you will be offered a private phone number to a sales coach where you can access him or her 24/7 for support.

On the business side of things CEOs, managers, and owners use our services to help grow, and scale their business. We help them with training to their employees and work with them on increasing sales revenue.

# -Business Branding & Leadership Development-

F inally, our leadership development program is for individuals looking for a raise in their current company or companies looking to promote people within their organization and want them to become better leaders. We teach you how to become a celebrity in your industry, how to be a national author, and make people want to follow you.

Some of the topics I'm going to discuss in this final piece is, why inspiration can cause problems not fix them. Why modesty is not an actual trait of leaders, and an interesting observation of why a leader in a wolf pack "eats first."

(15) Aside from execution, there are two ways to understand many leadership failings, 1) the "bad apple" theory. That an organization has simply done a bad job at selecting the right people for leadership roles. Those leaders themselves have developed bad values. 2) The process that produces leaders who often behave differently from what most people expect. Basically, the social

psychology that makes the actual trait and behaviors, that causes leaders to be successful in their careers and attain senior-level positions, are quite different from the qualities we hear about or desire in leaders.

We talk about leaders as; motivating, team people, willing to put others first, etc. But people are too focused on what leaders "should" do and how things "ought" to be, that they ignore the fundamental question of what actually is true. What is actually occurring and why?

When you hear Trump, Jobs, Gates, do those names sound like modest, or kind? Maybe they do today, years after. But when they were in the positions you are today, trying to build and grow. They were fierce, sharks, demoralizing, and cut throat.

We have to track and measure accountability for work place outcomes. You may "like" someone, but if they are not producing results, you need to make a change. By measuring and scoring, you focus attention and make problems salient. Also, evaluate your leaders on their ability to attract and retain talent. Measuring behavior in tough situations and measure implementation. Is your leader someone who people stick around for? Who people choose to work for?

We talk about motivation and inspirational leaders. The problem with this is that inspiration is temporary. You watch the movie Rocky and the rest of the day you are all pumped up. But tomorrow that feeling has dissipated. Sometimes motivation creates un-realistic expectations and can hurt the teams' overall morale in long term. Maybe by being cynical at times motivates people in the long term to actually make results. Maybe Donald Trump calling our leaders in the white house "incompetent" will in the long haul make them competent. Sometimes instead of sugarcoating someone's weight issues only makes the problem worse. Instead a true leader at times needs to say, "go to the gym now!" it may in that moment not feel good, but it could change that person's life, like Simon Cowell on American Idol.

When I was younger playing football, I was in 8th grade in our championship game. I had two touchdowns and 100+ yards rushing. By any standards I was having a spectacular performance. One play I fumbled the ball and my coach grabbed me on the sideline, picked me up and yelled at me so profusely I almost cried. Everyone else patted me on the back and said, "Don't worry your having a great game." But the moment my coach scolded me I never ever forgot that moment. I never let go of that ball again....it didn't feel good at the time but it made a lasting change.

The other thing leaders must do is be able to put on a show. To display energy and pay attention to others, regardless of how they personally feel at that moment in time.

As a CEO of thousands of people whom for the most part you may only see once in a while, it doesn't matter if you're sick, or pissed, when you are in front of them as a group. You must put on a show and be engaged for a brief moment of interaction. People must see you have energy both intellectually and physically to lead the company. For me personally, I am a quiet person, but in front of a group, in a presentation, or one-on-one I am superman instead of Clark Kent.

You have heard, I'm sure about "Authentic Leaders." In our leadership development program, we teach that leaders don't need to be authentic. Leaders need to be true to what the situation is and to what those around them want and need.

The sociologist Arlie Hochschild has written about emotions. Front line people like sales agents, flight attendants, employees at Disney World, are all called upon to display positive emotions that they might not be feeling at the time. "Emotion.... can be, and often is subject to acts of management. The individual often works on inducing or inhibiting feelings so as to render them "appropriate" to a situation.... meaning to put more premiums on the individual's capacity to do emotion-work."

I want to go back to modesty for a moment. As Jeffery Pfeiffer discussed in his book Leadership BS, Donald Trump is listed in Forbes as the 417th richest person in the world. In recent times, he got into a spat with Rahm Emanuel, the mayor of Chicago, when Trump put up a giant sign 200ft high on the ninety-six story Trump international hotel, Chicago's second tallest building. The sign says "Trump." Emanuel though that "this was an architecturally tasteful building scarred by an architecturally tasteless sign" (USA Today, June 13, 2014). Trump is also stated by the Wall St. Journal as "Puffery, pushiness, and deception." But one thing the Donald has done for sure is build a brand worth billions. His job is to sell hotel rooms, casino experience, and living quarters in competitive markets and now, to be the 45th President of the United States.

History has many examples of this. The most conceded and self-confident people, whether or not it's deserved, always seem to rise to the leadership role quickest.

However, modesty has its part. Most leaders are less likely to claim credit for the accomplishments of others, and more prone to acknowledge what others have done. People are unlikely to work as hard for "your" project or "the boss's project" as they are for "our" project.

My dad is great at this. He always makes everyone feel as though it's everyone's success. That is what good leaders do. But at the same time, it is about self-promotion. This is called implicit egotism. This is the idea that we all like things that remind us of ourselves. Basically, because we like ourselves, we will like things that remind us of ourselves. The next principal is the endowment effect, which is basically a how and why we have a higher value for what we have simply because it's ours.

In our leadership development course, we will go into greater depth. But to end this paragraph, I want to list leaders who would be considered egotistical and narcissistic: Bill Gates, Steve Jobs, Jack Welch of General Electric, John D. Rockefeller, Robert Johnson of BET, David Geffen of DreamWorks, Michael Eisner of

Disney, Walt Disney, and numerous politicians, Joseph Stalin, George Bush.

These traits help attain leadership position in the first place, and then once in them it positively effects their ability to hold the position.

There are lines between what you should do and what needs to be done. Our program will cover everything from start to finish and over the course of 12 months you will have the knowledge, the branding material, and the self-confidence you need to be a leader. Weather it's for a job promotion, new hire, or you're a women looking to get equal pay for your position. You will network with others in this program and you will have a personal situation consultant available by phone to help you with a question of judgement.

Thank you for reading this book. I know there are many things left untouched. Visit our website and I wish you all a very successful future.

"In bocca al lupo, crepi il lupo."
"In the mouth of the wolf, may the wolf die."

Answers to MIT Study on page 32

1.  Bat $1.05

    Ball $0.05      (1.05 - .05 = $1.00 More)

2.  I Minute: Just because you add machines, doesn't mean longer time.

3.  Day 47: If it doubles each day, day 47 would be half.

Overview

Wealth Creator Clinic, Inc.

- ❖ Strategic Planning (Subscription)
  - 2-Day live Boot Camp
  - 4 Period planning sessions per year
  - Member Log-in to software program
  - Discounts for companies with 10+ Staff
  - As a member, you receive discount on personal coaching
- ❖ Business, Sales, & Executive Coaching ($500 mo. Individual, $200 mo. 10+ Group)
  - ½ Hour – 1 Hour per week coaching
  - Weekly accountability & score keeping
  - Psychology of a sale/customer
  - Sales, training scripts, and videos
  - Case preparation
  - Personal style and branding creation
  - Start-up or turn around support
- ❖ Business Branding & Leadership Experience ($30,000)
  - 12 Month experience to brand yourself or company as celebrities/experts in your industry
  - 4 Destination experiences
  - Learn how to attract & retain competent staff & customers
  - Brand to attract higher fees or compensation
  - Learn how to influence people to follow you

- Become nationally bestselling author
- Network with other business owners and executives
- Gain a powerful "super group" of Board of Directors to guide your business and personal visions.

Companies and individuals choose to join Wealth Creator Clinic because of the execution strategies and the companies vision for your future. What this means to you, is we will show you how to bridge your opportunities into reality, and guide you to a brighter future. However, the real benefit is the confidence, certainty, and peace of mind in knowing you are building the company and life you've always dreamed of.

Antonio is available for keynote and private coaching. Please visit the websites today for current pricing, availability and upcoming events.

www.antoniombravata.com

www.wealthcreaterclinic.com

# Notes:

## Be Do Have

A BE-Do-HAVE list is your wants and desires for who you want to be, what you want to do, and the things you wish to have.

Remember you can't get where you want to go unless you visualize it first:

## BE          DO          HAVE

Ex: Good Father_____Visit Italy_____$1M home__

_____

_____

_____

_____

_____

_____

_____

_____

_____

_____

_____

_____

_____

_____

_____

_____

# 3 & 5 Year Visions

## 3 Year Vision:

_____

_____

_____

_____

_____

_____

_____

_____

_____

_____

## 5 Year Vision:

_____

_____

_____

_____

_____

_____

_____

_____

_____

_____

## Source Page

1. Devils in Exile- Chuck Hogan

2. Why Money is Important- Dr. Drew Henry

3. Cashflow Quadrant: Guide to Financial Freedom- Robert T. Kiyosaki

4. The Warren Buffet Way- Robert G. Hagstrom

5. Thinking Fast and Slow- Daniel Kahneman

6. Copy Right, New York Life, Richard K. Stivers

7. Berkshire Hathaway Annual Report- Warren Buffett, 2005

8. The Intelligent Investor- Benjamin Graham

9. The Warren Buffet Way- Robert G. Hagstrom

10. The Warren Buffet Way- Robert G. Hagstrom

11. The Warren Buffet Way- Robert G. Hagstrom

12. The Warren Buffet Way- Robert G. Hagstrom

13. The Warren Buffet Way-Robert G. Hagstrom

14. Kelly Optimization Model- John Larry Kelly, Jr.

15. The Warren Buffet Way- Robert G. Hagstrom

16. The Warren Buffet Way- Robert G. Hagstrom

Please Pay Attention to

WWW.WEALTHCREATORCLINIC.COM

FOR UPDATES ON NEW BOOKS AND CONTENT


COMING SOON


SWIMMING UP STREAM – LAW OF A LEADER

BY: ANTONIO M. BRAVATA

www.ingramcontent.com/pod-product-compliance
Lightning Source LLC
Chambersburg PA
CBHW030003190526
45157CB00014B/403